CW01024925

RAYS OF
KNOWLEDGE

JASON SHURKA

Foreword written by Christiane Northrup, MD.

RAYS OF KNOWLEDGE: SACRED KNOWLEDGE REVEALED

1405 SW 6th Avenue • Ocala, Florida 34471 • Phone 352-622-1825 • Fax 352-622-1875
Website: www.atlantic-pub.com • Email: sales@atlantic-pub.com
SAN Number: 268-1250

Library of Congress Control Number: 2021911815

Printed in the United States

PROJECT MANAGER: Crystal Edwards
INTERIOR LAYOUT AND JACKET DESIGN: Nivash Prabakaran

DEDICATION

I would humbly like to dedicate this book to the brave souls who have dedicated their lives, and in some cases even risked their lives, to make this world a better place through the dissolution of evil and the elevation of collective awareness.

CONTENTS

The Beginning

Insights

ACKNOWLEDGMENTS

First and foremost, I would like to thank the Source of all Energy for blessing me with the path of life that I have experienced thus far. I have endless gratitude for the sacred information and experiences I have been allowed to receive, even though these may be overwhelming at times. I take no credit for anything I have done thus far because part of what the divinity of this limitless universe, along with my journey, has taught me is that "I" am not "me." "I" am simply the universe acting through "me."

Thank you for allowing the ever-present, omnipotent, and eternal Light to flow through everything and every being so effortlessly. Although I am the author of this book, I am not the creator of its content. I am simply the messenger of very valuable information and knowledge that I have acquired over the past few years, and for that, I am grateful. Thank you for making this book possible.

To my beloved friend who would like to remain anonymous—you know who you are. You are an absolute blessing in my life. You have blessed me with access to information and experiences that I could not have even begun to fathom a few years ago. Thank you for believing in me, supporting me, trusting me, and loving me. Thank you for constantly helping me realize my true power. Thank you for guiding me, even though I may be stubborn sometimes. Thank you for being the greatest mentor I could ask for. I look forward to what the future of our relationship holds. My feeling is that this is just the beginning. Thank you, my friend. I love you deeply.

To my beloved family, thank you for showing me the support that you do. Without it, I would not be able to fulfill what I am doing today. No matter how difficult my journey becomes, you are always there to remind me that I am not alone. Thank you for the unconditional love that you all embrace me with.

To my dearest soul friend, Talia, thank you for being one of the brightest lights in my life. You are my best friend, my second mother, and my teacher whom I truly love with no limits. Your loyalty and unconditional love have opened up my heart in ways that are truly incomprehensible to me. Thank you for being you. I love you!

To my dear friend Damien Wynne, your humility has taught me wonders. I will forever hold a special place for you in my heart. Thank you for being here for me even during my most difficult times. The patience and love you show me have propelled me to incredible heights.

To a new member of my soul family, Dr. Christiane Northrup, I am beyond grateful that you and I have crossed paths in this reincarnation. Coming in contact with you warmed my heart because I saw it as a clear indication from the universe that I am heading in the right direction. You are a true warrior of Light whom I look up to and admire in many ways. Thank you so much for all the brave work you do to wake up the world!

To my soul family Anton, Michael, Larry, Iviko, Malka, Megan, Yaniv and Liran, thank you all for supporting me and standing by my side no matter what. You have all played roles in shaping the emotional and mental strength I have developed over the past few years, and for that, I am grateful.

I love you all unconditionally and I am grateful to know your souls in this reincarnation.

FOREWORD

When I was about 12 years old, I was babysitting at the home of family friends. There was a small, unopened box on the table with the title *Natives of Eternity* on the cover in bold black letters. The box had come in the mail and was unopened. A quintessential "good girl," I next did something that astounds me to this day. I opened the box and took out the book inside.

Something inside me compelled me to commit this small crime of opening and reading someone else's mail. I simply had to see what that title meant. And it changed my life. Inside was a copy of Rev. Flower

Newhouse's book *Natives of Eternity*. It was about angels and devas and nature spirits. And there were pictures of them, drawn by an artist who could see them. I was so excited! In that moment, I realized that everything I ever hoped was true was in fact true.

We live in a magical universe in which unseen beings oversee the growth of every flower, every human, every animal. And more than that, nature is alive with nature spirits, devas of the wind, fire, and sea, angels of birth and angels of death teaming with them. And their sole purpose is to uplift and enlighten Mother Earth and her inhabitants, to let us know who they really are.

Once I read *Natives of Eternity* and saw the pictures, I knew, deep inside, that we are never alone, that there is always support. And I knew, most importantly, that there is far more to reality than we have been told. I have since carried this knowledge into medical school, an ob/gyn residency, the operating room, the delivery room, and my daily life. And this is why, when Jason Shurka asked me to write this foreword for *Rays of Knowledge*, I didn't hesitate. The landscape of *Rays of Knowledge* is very familiar to me.

Back to *Natives of Eternity*. When I got home, I told my mother what I had done. But I also conveyed my excitement. She called Gretchen, the woman at whose house I had been babysitting. And together they not only bought me my own copy (which I still have to this day), but also supported me in meeting Gretchen for brunch on a regular basis throughout my teenage years, to talk about angels and other mystical topics. She herself had met Rev. Newhouse, the author of *Natives of Eternity*, and had been to the Christward Ministry in California.

And thus began my education in metaphysics, angels, reincarnation, past lives, and medical intuition. I read every book I could get my hands on about Edgar Cayce, the "sleeping prophet" and one of the most famous medical intuitives in the world. I read all the novels of Joan Grant from her Far Memory series. *Winged Pharaoh*, first published in 1937, was one of my favorites. Grant wrote a series of novels based on her past lives. She was often taken on archaeological digs and was able to accurately identify the objects that were found and explain what they were used for.

In medical school and during my residency, I continued to be enthralled with metaphysical teachings, particularly the work of Joseph Whitfield, who wrote *The Treasure of El Dorado* and *The Eternal Quest*. But I had to keep this interest hidden because mainstream medicine and science were not open to any kind of information other than what can be referred to as "Newtonian cause-and-effect linear left-brained knowledge"—things you can measure with instruments that only work in a three-dimensional reality. This can be summarized by a comment from one of my colleagues back in medical school: "I can't believe that a woman of your intelligence could believe in angels."

I knew that my colleague was wrong, but I also knew that this person had more power in that world than I did. And so I, like so many of you, did what I had to do to fit in and get along. I kept still about what I really believed, unless I found myself in a supportive environment.

Still, the evidence supporting another way of thinking was all around me. For example, The Heisenberg uncertainty principle, which I learned in physics, proved beyond a shadow of a doubt that the consciousness of an observer in any experiment actually changes the results. In other words, human thoughts and emotions have very physical effects on matter. Werner Heisenberg himself said: "Not only is the universe stranger than we think, it is stranger than we *can* think."

But we've all been taught that this kind of thinking is dangerous. And history shows that it has indeed been dangerous for many people. Consider the nine million women who were burned as witches in the Middle Ages. Those witch trials went on for 300 years and contributed greatly to the economy of old Europe. Those so-called "witches" were herbalist midwives, and those with intuitive gifts. Nothing more. The shadow of what are known as "the burning times" lives on in our lives today, which is why Joseph Campbell, the esteemed author of *The Hero's Journey*, once said: "The function of orthodoxy is to create martyrdom for mystics."

I had my very first astrological reading in the early 1980s. The astrologer, who was also very psychic, told me: "Someday I'm going to have a cocktail party and invite all of you doctors who consult me but don't dare talk about it to each other. You'll get to see how many of you there really are."

Given the current worldview of those who have been in power for centuries, is it any wonder that Jason Shurka's friend Ray, whose affiliation with The Light System (TLS) was the inspiration for this book, doesn't want the world to know who he is? It was the same with Joseph Whitfield, mentioned earlier, who wrote under a pseudonym. He also preferred to remain anonymous to protect himself and his family. The jacket description of *The Eternal Quest* reads in part: "*The Eternal Quest* will also challenge you to reconsider your concepts of marriage, extraterrestrial human life, reincarnation, life after death, good and evil, and the unseen worlds and dimensions and even the nature of God."

So, what is it about esoteric knowledge about our true power as humans that is so dangerous to the status quo? Why should Ray worry about having his name associated with this book, or others? Why did I feel the need to hide all my metaphysical books from my former husband, a Harvard-trained orthopedic surgeon? How is it that the practice of medicine quite deliberately leaves out the soul—and appears to take great care to get people to believe that their health is not connected with their thoughts, feelings, emotions, behavior, and diets? What is really going on here? You'll find answers to that in *Rays of Knowledge.*

As a board-certified ob/gyn with decades of clinical practice that have also included being a professor of ob/gyn and teaching medical students, creating eight highly successful public television specials, and writing three *New York Times* best-selling books, I am all too familiar with censorship and how the mainstream medical system has always censored information on natural remedies like vitamin C and homeopathy, yet champions expensive drugs and multiple vaccines as the only answers to health. Why is it that, with all my mainstream credentials and achievements, I felt compelled to simply give back my medical license so that I could speak freely about what I know to be true, rather than risk public censure?

Think about it. We doctors, with impeccable training in the best medical schools in the world, can't speak freely about the incredible benefits of high-dose vitamin C to fight infection. We are not allowed to question—even among colleagues—the wisdom of giving children 69 mandated vaccines from birth to age 18. Many have simply lost the ability to think critically.

So how in the world is one supposed to talk about angels, reincarnation, past lives, and so many of the other mysteries that affect our health? I'll tell you how: by opening your mind to the truth that has been hidden from us for centuries. We humans are far more than we realize. We are exquisitely creative, skilled, and compassionate. And we are fueled by the power of love. Right now, the human race is in a birth canal and in hard, messy labor. We are birthing a whole new consciousness onto planet Earth. Those of us—like Jason Shurka, the author of this and other books—who have been studying metaphysics and energy for years are acting as planetary midwives for this birth. It is not easy. But as more and more of us awaken to who we really are, it will get easier and easier for others.

This book that you now hold in your hands contains long-hidden information that can help free you from the prison of your own education and indoctrination—indoctrination based on systems of control and domination that have enslaved humanity for centuries but which are now crumbling all over the planet. It can awaken within you the experience of your own divine nature and remind you of your own power as a fully sovereign being. If you have read this far, I guarantee you that you are the one you have been waiting for. Your light and your power are flowing back to you right now. And as you read on, more and more of your wisdom will come through to you via Jason's story and words. Welcome to the New Earth.

—Christiane Northrup, M.D.

"If I have seen further than others, it is by standing upon the shoulders of giants."

—Isaac Newton

INTRODUCTION

Have you ever just observed the world around you in a state of complete presence and deep observation, without necessarily needing to identify what it is that you are observing? If you are unsure of what I am referring to, take a look at any part of your body.

I invite you to take a look at your hand, only this time don't identify it as your hand that has five fingers, fingernails, and skin. Just look at it for what it truly is. In a state of pure presence and deep observation, consciously look at the shape of your hand, the feel of your skin, the texture of your fingernails. Try to lose the idea that what you are looking at is a "hand"

and simply see it for what it *is* instead of what you have been taught to identify it as. You will come to a point in your present observation where you will see and experience your hand differently than you have ever seen it before! The moment we attach an identification to something, we lose sight of its true nature. We, the human race, have lost sight of our own true nature as spiritual and energetic beings.

Most of us are so caught up in the matrix of life that we tend to cultivate low-vibrational programming instead of wonder and curiosity. Doing so keeps us in a state of spiritual suppression. Throughout history, leading up to this very day, the human race has followed an upward trend of becoming mentally and spiritually enslaved and suppressed. We, the human race, have forgotten what it truly means to be human. We've lost sight of our true nature to a point that we now call the natural "supernatural" because information and knowledge have been kept from us. Books have been burned, and digital information has been censored. Our true power is being kept hidden from us!

Although there is a growing community of souls who are waking up, the majority of our race is still asleep. What makes waking up even harder is the fact that those who are still asleep ridicule and criticize those who dare open their eyes. Why? Because those who open their eyes come to realize that what they thought was true in their sleeping state (unconscious and unaware) could not have been further from the truth in their awakened state (conscious and aware). On the other hand, the sleepers live in a state of programming and identification. They live in the matrix. The sleepers believe they are what they identify to be and when one has the privilege of waking up—which is usually a very uncomfortable journey of evolution and growth—they come to understand that reality is not what they always thought it was. The reason why the sleepers ridicule those who dare open their eyes is because their realizations of the true nature of our world shake and threaten the entire foundation of anybody who is still asleep.

The year 2020 was clearly a quite uncomfortable year for humanity on a global scale. We are living in unprecedented times. Fear has been instilled into the public, the global economy has come crashing down, the civil rights of many have been stripped away, and the entire world has broken into chaos. However, there has also been a great awakening on a global scale. I did say it is usually a very uncomfortable journey of evolution and growth, didn't I?

On the individual level, waking up usually occurs once an individual hits rock bottom. Why? Because no one wants to make a change if they don't have to! Well, we are experiencing the beginning of hitting rock bottom, only now it is on a collective level of experience. Many sleepers have been forced to open their eyes and accept certain realities about the world that we live in that they couldn't even begin to fathom a year ago. Truth is prevailing time and time again, and the divine design of the universe and our experience of reality within it are becoming more apparent every day.

The purpose and intention behind writing book is to further facilitate the process of waking up, to make the process more comfortable and exciting. Waking up becomes much easier when knowledge is sprinkled into the process. Without knowledge, which is true power, waking up can become a very uncomfortable and bumpy road. My intention is not to facilitate the process of waking up through pressure, force, and fear, but through knowledge, experience, compassion, and love! After all, being awake simply means being conscious and aware, and being conscious and aware of knowledge that may have been suppressed is where the key to our true power exists.

In other words, it all begins with awareness. A higher level of awareness is what will eventually lead us to collectively understand that what we call "supernatural" is actually natural! We must always remember that consciousness and awareness have no limits! So, even if you feel that your eyes are open, there is always more to learn and a higher level of awareness and consciousness to reach. The beauty of the information contained within this book is that it is not just for the sleeper, but also for those who consider themselves awake.

The information you are about to read is dense and powerful, and at times may even feel overwhelming. My advice is to listen to your soul and read it all at your own pace, no matter how slow or fast that pace may be. The following information is a consolidation of some of the experiences and valuable information that I have acquired either through firsthand experience or through receiving it from a dear friend of mine, who is affiliated with a very powerful undercover organization known as

The Light System, or TLS. The information in this book covers a wide array of subjects, insights, and spiritual secrets, such as:

1. The revelation of an underground and omnipotent organization known as The Light System (TLS) along with who they are, their ultimate purpose, and why they chose to reveal themselves now after thousands of years of existence.

2. Information and insights from a high-vibrational book known as *Rays of Light*, which is currently in the possession of its original author, who refuses to publish it in its entirety for reasons I will explain.

3. Current and upcoming ages that we are experiencing, and will experience, on a universal scale such as the "Age of Light" and "The Age of Love."

4. Insights from a high-vibrational document known as "The Pyramid Code" containing very valuable information, which was released to the public for the first time on September 9, 2020 (9/9/2020) at 9 a.m. EST. These insights include why this document was given to the public at this moment in time, the truth behind the beings who built the pyramids, the technology used to build the pyramids, the operational functions of the pyramids, the power behind the shape and numerology of the pyramids, the true criteria for life, and much more.

5. Knowledge regarding the spiritual suppression and enslavement of the human race, along with many examples of how and why this suppression is implemented.

6. In-depth details and insights regarding extraterrestrial life on other planets, including

their biological features, how they live, the technology they possess, their level of awareness, their intentions of coming to Earth, their work with TLS, and much more.

7. The true importance of planet Earth in this vast universe, in both the physical and the spiritual planes.

8. Knowledge from a very high and powerful source that will shed light on how one can raise not only their vibration of being but the collective vibration of being as well, through mediums such as food, thought, intention, and action.

9. In-depth knowledge and insights regarding fifth-dimensional awareness, which will help dissolve the illusions that the human race lives by in order to help the human race transcend to a higher level of awareness.

Whether you are a "sleeper" or an "awakening one," I understand that some of the information contained within this book may challenge your current belief system. I invite you to let go of the idea that you are your beliefs. Doing so may make it easier to let go of them and digest the following information with no bias, filter, or lens. None of the information contained within this book is channeled information.

All the information and insights contained herein are derived from physical experiences. I want to remind you all of one very important thing: All the information contained within this book is not just "based on a true story," but it *is* a true story. What you choose to do with this information is up to you! Those who are ready to receive this information will not just believe, but they will know that the information contained within this book is absolutely true. My intention in publishing this book is not to persuade the reader of the validity of the information that exists within it. My intention is simply to plant the very necessary seeds of knowledge and awareness that I am sure will sprout and flourish when humanity, as a whole, is ready.

I am aware that many people may call me a fraud, and that is okay. I hope it is clear at this point that I don't see publishing this information and knowledge as a choice. I understand the strength it holds in energetically raising the vibration and level of awareness of humanity, which is why I see it as an absolute obligation, regardless of how some may perceive me as a result of doing so. I don't believe that I have the right to hold back such valuable information out of the fear that others may look at me differently.

My experiences over the past two years have allowed me to understand that personal sacrifices must be made in order to bring humanity to a new level of awareness. And after all, I feel that is my purpose and my destiny here on Earth. Such sacrifices are the reason why I live. I would have no reason to be here if I was not aligned with my purpose and my destiny.

It is my belief that if you are currently reading this—although you may not be completely ready to absorb the information that you are about to read—you are most definitely ready to receive it. Otherwise, it would not have come into your possession to begin with. I ask you to read the following information, not just with an open mind, but most importantly, with an open heart. Allow yourself to step out of mind and logic, and into heart and love. Allow it to speak to your spirit and resonate with your soul. I wish us all the best of luck in our journey of reaching a higher level of awareness, a journey filled with light, peace, and love. May this information play a role in helping us unite as one, and most importantly, may it bring us one step closer to true bliss and the Age of Love.

And so, the journey begins…

THE BEGINNING

t all began on June 9, 2018, when I was approached by a man who had, and still has, incomprehensible depths of experience and knowledge, a man whose presence in my life started as a stranger and has evolved into an unbreakable bond. Our interaction started as an interesting conversation and evolved over time into something much more than that. This man possesses a vast amount of valuable information and sacred knowledge that could be critically useful for us all on a universal level.

Today I know that this man's appearance in my life was no coincidence. Our friendship began with some interesting conversations that got deeper as our relationship progressed. Over time, as our relationship grew stronger, he revealed more and more information to me, until he finally revealed his affiliation with a very powerful, undercover, and divine organization that has been in existence for thousands of years, known as The Light System (TLS). It is my biggest honor to have been appointed by TLS to be the individual to bring their existence, along with a lot of other valuable information, to the awareness of the public.

I believe that he, along with the TLS organization, has blessed me with the opportunity of sharing this valuable information with the world for several reasons. First and foremost, I believe that the information contained within this book will provide whoever reads it access to a higher level of awareness and consciousness that will be necessary in the near future, for reasons that I will address shortly.

Second, it is my understanding that I am being prepared to publish a very important and high-vibrational book, also written by this man, called *Rays of Light*, which is an 864-page book filled with sacred insights and wisdom regarding the true nature of the universe that we live in. (More information regarding *Rays of Light* will be addressed shortly.)

Another reason I believe I was given the honorable task of being able to share all this information publicly is because he refused to do this himself. I understand that he would like to remain anonymous in order to avoid dealing with the many people who may perceive him as insane, and in order to protect his family and others. This is quite understandable, considering the magnitude of the information without hard evidence to back it all up. For purposes of simplicity, I will refer to him as "Ray" from here on, in order to preserve his anonymity.

However, please note that Ray is not his real name. Ray made it very clear that, although he is aware the information he possesses is quite valuable and will play a big role in raising and shifting the vibration of the collective consciousness here on Earth, he would rather let it all be exposed either by somebody else or after his death in order to not have to deal with the consequences (both positive and negative) of revealing such information.

For the reasons I have just stated, and probably many others I am not aware of, I was asked to be that "somebody else."

It is my wish and hope that, in time, I will be able to convince Ray to come forward and reveal all the documents, information, and codes that are in his possession and in the possession of TLS, in order to share these with the masses. I respectfully request from every individual who may be aware of his true identity to respect his wish to preserve his anonymity for now, so we shall have a better chance of inducing him to reveal more information in the future.

Additionally, I would like to use this opportunity to implore TLS and my dear friend Ray to come forward and exercise full transparency and reveal any and all information—past, present, and future—for our sake and for the sake of the greater good!

Over the last couple of years, I have been going through a disclosure process, in which Ray has slowly given me access to very valuable and powerful information, as I was prepared to receive it. This information includes the revelation of a very powerful organization that I now know as The Light System (TLS), insights and knowledge of the spirit world, his in-depth knowledge and experiences with extraterrestrial life, his in-depth memories from both distant as well as more recent reincarnations, information regarding existing high technology that is not available to the public domain, spiritual secrets, secrets of planet Earth, and much more that will be elaborated on in this book.

The beauty of how I received this information lies within the divine process of disclosure that I am still going through. I received only what I was ready to receive, whether it was information or a physical experience. Looking back, I am most grateful for the process of disclosure I have gone through—and that I am still experiencing—because this is what is keeping me sane and balanced on a physical, emotional and spiritual level.

Although I received information in such divine timing, I still had my doubts, and rightfully so. The information shared with me was quite extraordinary and unbelievable. However, much of it made sense to me, due to the foundation of knowledge I have cultivated over the years. Growing up, I was always fascinated by the supernatural and spiritual realms and dimensions of the universe. Subjects including extraterrestrial life, the pyramids, levitation with the body, high technology, and spirituality have always interested me deeply. Despite the fact that the information made somewhat logical sense to me, it was still extremely difficult to believe and fully comprehend.

However, that all changed on the evening of February 6, 2020. On that evening, I had a firsthand experience that confirmed and validated all the information I have been blessed with over the past two years. I will elaborate on what occurred on the evening of February 6, in limited detail, shortly.

My journey has become public as of September 9, 2020, when TLS gave me permission to release a document entitled "The Pyramid Code" to the public, along with a lot of other valuable information. Ever since, my entire life has shifted completely. In just a short period of time, the document has been downloaded by hundreds of thousands of people around the world. I have been asked to do TV shows, documentaries, and public interviews with prominent and respected public figures from all around the world.

Contrary to what most people think, sharing this information with the world has not been an easy task. Over the past few months, as my public presence gained more traction, I have been called every name under the sun—from the best to the worst—by strangers, friends, and even my own family: a saint, an angel, and a messiah, all the way to a liar, a fraud, and a mentally ill human being.

I want to make one thing clear: I am none of the above. I am not a messiah, nor a saint. I am not an angel nor a guru. I am not a liar nor a fraud. I have nothing to do with any of the names, both good and bad, that people have associated with me.

So allow me to give you a brief background of who I am. My name is Jason Shurka, and I am 24 years old. I was born and raised in New York. I graduated from the Zicklin School of Business at Baruch College in New York City, and I work in commercial real estate for a living. I'm a simple man with simple needs. I am a normal person who has been asked to fulfill an incredible task, which is nothing but my honor to do. I am nothing more than a messenger of information. I was approached and given instructions to bring TLS and specific information to the public. I didn't have to say yes—I chose to say yes! I chose to say yes because what kind of person would I be if I held such valuable information and didn't share it out of fear of what others might think about me? So, here I am today, a normal person fulfilling an incredible task. That's who I am, and that's all I am.

THE LIGHT SYSTEM (TLS)

So what is TLS? The Light System (TLS) is a very powerful, undercover, and divine organization. You can think of TLS as a spiritual version of the Central Intelligence Agency (CIA), only much more powerful and within divine intentions.

Their ultimate purpose is to help assist and guide humanity in reaching a higher level of awareness and consciousness, without intervening with the natural process of humanity's conscious evolution. Although I am not aware of exactly what year TLS was formed, I do know that the organization has existed for more than 5,000 years. After a very long existence in the shadows, TLS has decided to reveal themselves for who they are, what they do, and why they do it. I am beyond honored to have been appointed for the task of bringing their existence, among a lot of other valuable information, to the awareness of the public.

The existence of TLS was first revealed to the public on August 26, 2020, in an interview (in which I took part) with George Noory on Coast to Coast AM Radio. This is the first time in history that information about TLS is being published in a book for the public to read. (Of course, permission from TLS has been granted in advance.)

At this point (as of May 2021), it is important for you to know that I am not initiated into the organization. I have just been approached, prepared, and appointed as a messenger of information by TLS. However, if the time for initiation ever does come up, and providing the conditions are appropriate, it would be my absolute honor to be initiated into this divine organization.

TLS has branches in every major city in the world. Every branch has a general manager, who could be either male or female, who is in charge of overseeing operations for that division of the organization. Each "branch" and/or "division" is referred to as a "chapter." For example, the current head of the New York chapter of TLS is an older woman. TLS is made up of roughly 7,000 initiated agents around the world, some of whom are very well-known people in the modern world. Some are in the government, others are in the media, as celebrities, producers, and so on. However, most initiated agents in TLS are not well known in the world.

Regardless whether an agent is known publicly or not, all initiated agents live double lives. Every agent who works in TLS is provided with a cover story to explain where they work and what they do. Yes, this means that your own mother or father could be a part of TLS, and you would have absolutely no idea. TLS has nothing to do with religion, race, age, or gender. In many cases, agents are chosen based on the energy they are born with, which is explained in the final chapter of this book.

The organization is made up of all religions, races, ages, and genders. When I say "all ages," I am also referring to human beings who are several hundreds of years old. For example, one of the leaders of TLS is more than 400 years old. However, the oldest man I know of in TLS (although I have not met him) is more than 600 years old. When I say "all races," I am referring to races that are not parts of the human race. Although it may sound unbelievable, not all initiated agents in TLS are human beings.

Yes, I am saying exactly what you think I am saying. There are extraterrestrials who work with TLS and who live among us today. We are not here alone. Contrary to popular belief, extraterrestrials are not here to hurt us or invade us. Rather, they are here to help us and guide us. They are here to help us reach a higher level of awareness and consciousness. I know of one who comes from a planet by the name of Konom. He is a very short (roughly 3 feet tall) alien-looking creature with damp and shiny, dolphin-like skin who has been trained to become a human being over the past few years and now looks like us through a holographic shapeshifting process that he had to go through, which I will explain in a later chapter. Today, he is a human being who lives on Earth and works with TLS. I will provide in-depth details regarding extraterrestrial life later on in this book.

TLS performs both physical and energetic/ spiritual tasks in every subject, plane, dimension, and geographical location in the universe (not just Earth). The tasks, in most cases, are complex group operations. However, there are instances where an agent is sent on a mission without any backup or support. All initiated agents in TLS get paid, though agents who work on the spiritual side of the organization are generally volunteers. Any agent who is paid for their work is paid by TLS under a different alias, which is generally connected to the cover story that the agent has for their day-to-day job.

TLS is a self-sufficient and financially independent organization that is not reliant on any donations in order to operate. The finances to pay their agents come from the many companies and businesses that they operate. I have received a common question asking if all TLS agents possess a high level of awareness and supernatural abilities. The simple answer is no—not all TLS agents possess a high level of awareness and supernatural abilities, though some do.

TLS has possession of and access to incredible high technology, some of which completely defies the laws of physics that are publicly known to modern-day physicists and scientists. I am referring to technology such as craft that can travel intergalactically within seconds, technology that has the power to heal the sick instantaneously, and much more. They are not an organization that is limited to the speed of light, because they can and they do transcend the dimensions of time and space.

Ultimately, TLS is a very unique, divine and omnipotent organization, and they are here to help guide and assist humanity in reaching a higher level of awareness and consciousness.

When it comes to TLS, I have received a common question from thousands of individuals around the world that I would like to address:

"If TLS is such a powerful organization that is here to help humanity, then why does our world look the way that it looks? Additionally, if TLS is such a powerful organization, then why don't they just eliminate the evil people and dark forces from our world so we can live in a world of peace and love after all?"

These are both great questions, and fortunately TLS has answers! First and foremost, it is important to understand that TLS is not responsible for humanity. Humanity is responsible for humanity. We are responsible for ourselves! TLS is simply here to help guide us along the way, in whatever way they can, without interfering with the natural process of evolution of the human experience. In order to understand the answer to the second part of the question, we must first understand a foundational principle:

The reality we are experiencing is a direct reflection of our consciousness and the frequencies that we are in resonance with. This means that the frequencies that we are in resonance with are a direct reflection of our consciousness. In other words, to change our reality, we must shift our consciousness.

What does this mean? This means that if we resonate on the same frequency as evil, then we will experience a reality where evil exists. However, if we resonate on a higher frequency than evil, such as peace and love, evil will not be able to exist in the first place, because reality is simply a reflection of what we are in resonance with. Evil exists in our world because we, the people, collectively resonate on a frequency that is in resonance with the same frequency that evil, and many other low-vibrational realities, exist on. This means that the evil in our world does not exist separately from us, but because of us.

To shift our reality, we must shift our consciousness. The reason TLS does not, and will not, focus on eliminating evil people and dark forces from our world overnight is because they understand that doing so would do absolutely nothing. Why? Well, let me ask you a question. If TLS were to eradicate the evil people and dark forces from the world overnight (and I am sure that they could, with the power they have), what would stop these evil people and dark forces from being replaced? The evil would simply be replaced with a different face behind the same low-vibrational frequency and resonance. Why? Because the issue was not dealt with from its root of creation: *consciousness and awareness of the masses.*

Collective consciousness and awareness are what dictate our resonance and vibration, and because of this, it is consciousness and awareness that dictate what exists in our reality. So long as our consciousness and awareness are in resonance with low-vibrational realities such as evil, corruption, and greed, no elimination or eradication of these forces from even the most powerful sources will be able to shift our reality into one where these realities don't exist. It is simply against the energetic laws of the universe.

TLS understands that the power to change this world is not through the elimination and eradication of evil and darkness, but through the education and elevation of awareness and consciousness of us, the masses. TLS focuses on educating and elevating the collective vibration of the masses with the intention of helping humanity shift out of resonance with low-vibrational realities, such as evil, thus not giving evil room to exist in our reality in the first place, and therefore dissolving these low-vibrational realities from their roots. Our shift into a new age for humanity will not come from the physical elimination of evil people and dark forces, but by an energetic shift of our collective consciousness that will occur through education, awareness, higher consciousness, knowledge, unification, compassion, and love!

WHY NOW?

Why is all of this information only being revealed now? According to TLS, we are now in an era called "The Age of Light." The Age of Light started on a famous date that many of us know as the end of the world: December 21, 2012. However, it wasn't the end of anything, but the beginning of a new era and a new age that we are currently experiencing today known as The Age of Light. This is an age of higher consciousness where things like meditation, mindfulness, and veganism are becoming more mainstream and accepted. These higher-vibrational activities are becoming part of the collective vibration of being on a global scale. Many have asked me how we can be sure that the collective is truly shifting into a higher vibrational state of awareness and consciousness.

Well, one of the easiest places to find an indication of such a shift is in the stock market. Over the past few years, several companies that specialize in plant-based meat substitutes have become publicly traded companies in the stock market that are worth billions of dollars. A multibillion-dollar valuation on a plant-based company is a reflection that demand is changing, and a change in demand is a direct reflection of a change in consciousness! Just a few years ago in the United States, it used to be nearly impossible to find vegan options anywhere outside of New York City, Miami, or Los Angeles. Today, it is becoming the norm for restaurants to have vegan or gluten-free options. Why? Because our collective consciousnes shifting, which therefore creates a collecr in what we choose to consume.

According to TLS, the next age that we are approaching is called "The Age of Love." This is an age in which our world will look completely different, for the better. Imagine living in a world without time and space, without walls, without borders, without wars, without disease, without toxins, without drugs, and without doctors. A world without false religious leaders. A world without corrupt lawyers, judges, or politicians. A world of love, brotherhood, harmony, and justice. A world of happiness, wealth, eternal abundance, and equality. The Age of Love is all of this, and more! An age of unification instead of division. An age where levitation, flight with the body, and intergalactic communication with other races in the universe is not supernatural but very natural. An age where every being in existence is in resonance with fifth-dimensional awareness or higher. This is the new age that TLS is assisting and helping humanity each through many different mediums.

According to TLS, our deadline of reaching this new age is exactly 180 years from December 21, 2012, which equates to December 21, 2192. The Age of Love is the collective destiny of all life in the universe that we will reach unconditionally. This means that no matter what evil forces may try to keep us suppressed and take us down, nothing will be able to hinder us from reaching this new age of awareness and consciousness. The question is, what will happen along the path to reaching this collective destiny, The Age of Love? TLS is simply here to help guide and assist us in reaching this new age of awareness and consciousness with as little damage as possible along the way.

This means that the avoidance of war, violence, and bloodshed is always preferred. My ultimate motivation for sacrificing my name and reputation by sharing this information with the world is the fact that we do not actually have to wait until the year

2192 in order to reach this new and beautiful age. If we act properly, take the guidance being offered to us, and raise our collective vibration through the unification of humanity and life as a whole, we can reach this new age much sooner, such as in our own lifetimes!

The truth is, I don't know how much faster the revelation of the information contained within this book will bring us to this new age, but I do know that it will most definitely bring us one step closer. And whether that one step equates to 10 minutes closer or 10 years closer, you better believe I will be standing behind it!

So, how does the revelation of information regarding TLS, the Age of Light, and the Age of Love help us? Beyond just revealing what TLS is, along with some of the information they hold, the awareness of their existence brings hope and faith to the reality that we will reach together—the reality of a unified consciousness among all life in the universe. There are good forces in play, and TLS is very much one of those forces. They are here to help us, assist us, and guide us. Most importantly, they are here to ensure that we do reach our collective destiny as humanity and life as a whole with as little damage as possible along the way. We will reach that time, we are already on our way, and TLS is most definitely with us every step of the way.

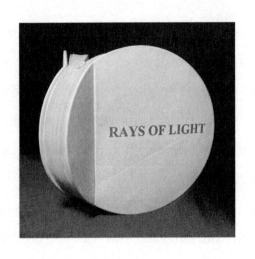

RAYS OF LIGHT

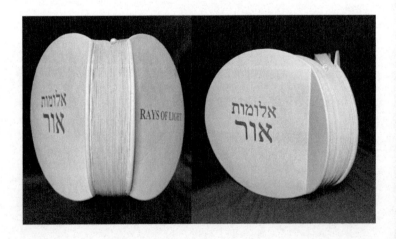

*R*ays of Light is an 864-page book with more than one million letters and symbols, written by Ray over the span of roughly four years between 2010 and 2014. The book is filled with spiritual insights, secrets of creation and the universe, in-depth knowledge regarding what many may consider to be "supernatural," powerful codes, and even proof to back it all up. *Rays of Light* is a consolidation of countless meetings between Ray and other members of TLS, along with in-depth experiences that he has had firsthand throughout his time working with TLS. The entire book was originally written by hand. Ray was given very special and high-vibrational water to drink throughout his handwritten documentations that helped him significantly raise his level of awareness to a state in which he could listen, speak, and write simultaneously at supernatural speeds.

In February of 2020, I was given 74 pages of the 864 pages to read. On October 10, 2020 (10/10/2020), I was given access to another 176 of the 864 pages to read, which is actually the first 176 pages of the entire book documented in the year 2010. To this day, I have read 250 of the 864 pages. Although I have not yet been given the privilege of reading the entire book, I am beyond grateful to have been given access to those 250 pages, as they have significantly expanded my mind, taught me deep and valuable lessons, and catalyzed my ascension process.

Rays of Light has been stored away in a secure safe for the past few years, waiting to be revealed to the world. Ray currently refuses to publish it because it contains a considerable amount of personal information about him, as well as a number of other people very close to him, including his wife and his family. Due to the sensitive, personal, and private information within *Rays of Light*, he is hesitant to publish the book, even though TLS has encouraged him countless times to do so. Despite his hesitation and objections to publishing the book, high-ranking members of TLS made clear to Ray that the book will eventually be published for the masses to read.

Rays of Light is encrypted with a code that is known to very few. Ray happens to be one of the few who has possession of the code. Without the code, one would simply read the book as a regular book with some incredible and unbelievable information and experiences. However, having possession of the code gives access to a whole other level of information, and even proof, that is contained within it. From my understanding, the revelation of this book *with* the codes will create a worldwide revolution and significantly help us shift to a higher level of consciousness and awareness.

Ray has agreed to publish *Rays of Light* under the condition that he is permitted to release it with the codes that unlock the true power that it holds. However, TLS has not permitted him to reveal the codes. Because of this, Ray simply prefers the book to be published after his death. And for whatever reason, he thinks that task will eventually become my responsibility. Whenever I try to convince him to see beyond his hesitation—and believe me, I try to push him a lot—he tells me time and time again that he does not want to deal with all the questions, as well as the great pressure that will come his way after the book is published. He also tells me that he sees no purpose in releasing *Rays of Light* without the revelation of the codes.

Additionally, there is some information that documents some of Ray's actions in the past that he is not very proud of, and he is afraid that revealing such information may harm him, along with his loved ones, if it is disclosed to the public at this point. He feels obligated to protect himself, those close to him, and his loved ones. Many people have asked me why Ray doesn't just change the names in the book and publish it anonymously, just as *The Pyramid Code* was published.

Originally, this was not an option, because one of the conditions imposed by TLS regarding the publication of *Rays of Light* is that it must be published "as is." However, that has all changed as of May 6, 2021. On that date, I was given permission to go through with the publication of the first 176 pages of *Rays of Light*, which, as I mentioned before, equates to the entire text documented in the year 2010. This was very exciting, as I did not expect such a revelation to occur in such a short period of time.

But I guess life is a dynamic journey full of surprises! As I've said many times in the past, it is my ultimate goal to convince Ray to publish the book in its entirety for the world to read—however, at this point he is not yet willing to do so.

Although I may not agree with Ray's actions, I cannot judge him because I understand where he is coming from, and truthfully I am not sure what I would do in his situation, since I'm not aware of everything he has gone through. I would like to think that I would put the greater good before myself, but I could never really know what I would do unless I were in his shoes. Ray is a normal middle-aged man who is known for his cover instead of who he truly is. He has a wife and kids. He is financially comfortable. He has made a beautiful life for himself! For him to come out with all this information and disclose his true identity would mean he would have to accept a major shift in his life. And according to him, he is just not ready to do that at this point in his life.

In my eyes, fear of what others think and a shift in an individual's life are insignificant in comparison to the world and the greater good, but the fact of the matter is that Ray feels otherwise, and those things are significant to him. Although I don't agree with his ways, I do respect him and his wishes.

Many people have approached me in complete confusion regarding the fact that Ray, a man who has reached such high spiritual places in life, still cares about low-vibrational realities such as the fear of being judged by others. From my experiences and from conversations I've had with many people over the past few months, I have found that many people have this idea that if an individual possesses "supernatural abilities," that individual must be a high-vibrational and spiritual Buddha-like being of light.

This could not be further from the truth! On the contrary, there are many people with supernatural abilities who use their powers for low-vibrational and evil acts. Although Ray has gained access to supernatural abilities (which we all possess) and has had experiences that many of us cannot even begin to comprehend, let alone fathom, he is a normal human being who experiences fear, judgment, and everything else under the sun, just like every one of us! Although *Rays of Light* in its entirety may not be released soon, I have been given permission to bring portions of information from the book (beyond the scope of the 2010 documentation) into this book, *Rays of Knowledge*, which is very exciting because of the power the information has to make a positive impact on anyone who receives it!

Please note that *Rays of Light* was originally written mostly in Hebrew, with only a few parts written in English, so many excerpts that I will bring into this book will simply be translations from the original. Furthermore, I have included two pictures of the table of contents of *Rays of Light*, one in the original Hebrew and one in the English translation. Please be aware than the table of contents in English that is included in this book is *not* a part of *Rays of Light*! It is simply a translation of the Hebrew version of the table of contents that *is* a part of the book.

TABLE OF CONTENTS

אלומות אור

מפתח עניינים

FEBRUARY 6, 2020

Something very significant happened to me on the evening of February 6, 2020 that confirmed and validated all the information I have been blessed with over the past 20 months leading up to that day. I had a firsthand experience that dissolved any doubts I had regarding the powerful information that Ray has shared with me.

On February 6, 2020 I was invited to an evening that included a dinner and a meeting afterward. There were six of us, including me and Ray. Following a beautiful and tasty dinner, we went into another room for a meeting. We started the evening at roughly 6 o'clock, and finished 12 hours later at roughly 6 o'clock in the morning. Although we were a party of six at dinner, we turned into a party of nine at the meeting, since three individuals joined us for it: Rabbi AA, along with two other individuals, one being the current head of the TLS New York chapter, and the other whom I am not at liberty to disclose.

Rabbi AA is a 424-year-old human being with immense spiritual and supernatural abilities. Although his full name is Rabbi Aliezer Alfrandi, members of TLS call him Rabbi AA for short, since those are his initials. Rabbi AA led the meeting as we all listened diligently. The two individuals who joined Rabbi AA for the meeting simply observed. Unfortunately, I cannot divulge too many details of what occurred that night. However, I will do my best to share what I can. At this point, it is important to reiterate that, although one of the leaders of the organization is a Jewish Rabbi, TLS has nothing to do with religion. As I mentioned before, TLS is made up of all religions, races, and ethnic groups.

Throughout the meeting, Ray and I, along with the other four individuals being spoken to in the meeting, were each given specific instructions. I was given a lot of clarity regarding a few topics in my life and was clearly shown my path in this reincarnation. I was given instructions regarding what to do as well as what not to do in order to reach and access this path. Rabbi AA gave me specific directions in order to prepare for a very important mission that I will have to fulfill sometime in the future.

These directions even included specific geographical locations of where and how to find specific sacred objects that will be revealed to the world when we are collectively ready. Ray's instructions were very significant as well because, ultimately, they are the reason why I have been given permission to write this book and include such valuable information within it in the first place! Rabbi AA gave Ray permission to share the in-depth memories that he holds from his first incarnation (which began in the year 1361 BC) with me and the other four individuals being spoken to at the meeting, under the condition that he also documents and shares the science and mysticism behind the pyramids with us as well.

Although Ray was confused about why sharing this information with us was a condition of sharing the in-depth memories he remembered from his first incarnation, he followed Rabbi AA's instructions as a sign of the high respect he holds for the rabbi. In order to clearly remember and document not only his first incarnation, but also the science and mysticism behind the pyramids, a deep state of concentration and focus was necessary. It took Ray a few months to complete the document before he shared it with us.

In June 2020, he completed the document and gave it to me to read, along with the other four individuals who were being spoken to in the meeting on February 6, 2020. I had to read it several times before I even began to understand the magnitude of what I was reading. Initially, I was under the impression that this document was allowed to be given only to the people who attended the meeting and had to remain confidential. However, after a short conversation with Ray, I understood that TLS gave him permission to publish the document for the public to read as well. I did my best to convince him to publish the information, but just as he did with the publication of *Rays of Light* in its entirety, he refused.

I was genuinely disappointed that I held such valuable information that was permitted to be shared with the world, but I couldn't share it all because Ray didn't want to reveal himself. And I was determined to do whatever it took to release this document to the public. After endless conversations, debates, and arguments, I finally succeeded. However, I succeeded in reaching an outcome that I could never have even imagined. After some time Ray said, "Okay, if you truly want to publish this information to the world, you do it. TLS is permitting to change the names in order to preserve my anonymity on this document. Change the names so no one can connect it back to me, make sure the author is anonymous, and publish it."

Honestly, I was caught completely off guard, but how could I say no to such an opportunity? What kind of person would I be if I refused to do what I tried encouraging Ray to do? What kind of person would I be if I refused to share valuable information with the world out of fear that others may think I am crazy? So, I embraced it wholeheartedly and with absolutely no hesitation. I released the document on my website for the public to download for free and share it with the world on September 9 at 9 o'clock in the morning (9/9/2020 at 9 a.m. EST) as TLS instructed me to do. Within the first three hours of the document going live on my website, it reached every continent on Earth, with the exception of

Antarctica. The document has been translated into eight different languages with the help of some incredible volunteers from all around the world. Ray was, and still is, pleasantly surprised. The document I am referring to is now known as "The Pyramid Code." It can be downloaded for free on my website at www.Jasonshurka.com.

THE PYRAMID CODE

"The Pyramid Code" is a 44-page, high-vibrational document containing very valuable information and spiritual insights. Ray, the man who has blessed me with the divine opportunity of receiving such valuable information, has been and will always be a big part of my journey into this new world of personal awareness and consciousness.

The information contained within the document is a true and accurate account of the beginning of his journey into the spirit world in his current reincarnation, his memories from a very important past reincarnation in ancient Egypt (which I happen to be a part of), his knowledge and wisdom of the sacred science and mysticism of the pyramids, as well as his knowledge of the new age toward which humanity is heading.

"The Pyramid Code" also covers the truth behind the beings who built the pyramids, the technology used to build the pyramids, the operational functions of the pyramids, the power behind the shape and numerology of the pyramids, the true criteria for life, spiritual secrets of reincarnation, and much more, with in-depth details. Please note that all the names in the document, with the exception of my own, have been changed in order to preserve Ray's anonymity. The only other name in the document that has not been changed is Rabbi AA (Rabbi Aliezer Alfrandi).

Ray hand-wrote the original document in Hebrew. The reason for this is simply that Ray is more fluent in Hebrew than in English, and therefore it was more comfortable for him to write the document in his native language. Additionally, it is important to understand that this is not a religious document, but a historical document. The reason I am bringing up this point is because much of the story Ray tells in "The Pyramid Code" revolves around the time period when the Hebrews became the Jewish people. This is simply because this is the part of history that he happened to be a part of in his first incarnation, and this is what he remembers.

If you do decide to read the document, my suggestion is that you read between the lines and pay more attention to the insights behind the story rather than the story itself. Since the document has already been released and can be downloaded for free on my website in several different languages, and for the purposes of this book, I will not focus on the story being told throughout the document, but rather on the insights within the document, which may not be apparent when reading it. My intention of doing so is to guide the reader in reaching a higher level of awareness and understanding of the document.

It is important for me to emphasize that although Ray wrote "The Pyramid Code" under the instructions of TLS, he was personally against the publication of the document at this moment in time, in addition to any other documents related to him and his work. On the other hand, TLS is completely in support of it. One of the many reasons that Ray is against the publication of this information is because he does not believe that people are ready yet, especially if he cannot release the document while also revealing the codes to unlock the true power that it holds. Just like *Rays of Light*, this document is encrypted with a code that is known only to a very few.

However, the code needed to unlock the true power of this document is much more complex than the one used in *Rays of Light*. According to

Ray, it takes roughly six months just to learn how to apply the code to access the true information that this document holds. Also, whoever possesses the code to this document will be able to extract more than a thousand pages of information from its current 44 pages (in English). At this point in time, I personally do not have access to the codes for *Rays of Light* or "The Pyramid Code." Just as with *Rays of Light*, Ray has agreed to publish "The Pyramid Code" under his name, provided he is permitted by TLS to release them with the codes revealed to unlock the powerful information that they hold. However, TLS has not yet permitted him to reveal the codes.

Although true access to these documents, with the codes, would reveal information that is very valuable in helping us reach a new level of awareness and a new age of consciousness, chaos and turmoil could break out if too much were given too soon. There must be a process of disclosure, on both the individual and collective level, in order to help the transition of consciousness and awareness run smoothly without chaos, destruction, bloodshed, and war.

On one hand, Ray does not feel that humanity is ready for the information that is contained within both *Rays of Light* and "The Pyramid Code." On the other hand, he is willing to release both as long as he is permitted to release them with their operational codes. I do not agree with this whatsoever. I believe that if too much is disclosed too soon, it can do more harm than good. In "The Pyramid Code," it clearly states that these codes used to be part of the collective consciousness, and that they were not secrets. However, as the leaders of the nations began to abuse their power and control the people, the codes were taken away from them and from the public as a whole.

This is a direct reflection of what is happening in our world today! There are many people at high levels of authority around the world who are abusing their power. If the same codes that were taken away from us due to the abuse of power were given back to us at this moment in time, I believe we would be setting ourselves up for a disaster. Collectively, I do not feel that we are ready to receive codes with such immense power, but I do feel that we are ready to receive the information without the codes. I feel that receiving the information is simply a part of the process of disclosure, which will bring us one step closer to living in a reality in which we will be ready to receive the codes on a collective level without the threat of chaos, destruction, and disorder breaking out.

Another reason why Ray does not support the publication of "The Pyramid Code" is because he knows and understands that the people who are mentioned in the document, who have worked with him in the past and are close to him, will most likely realize his identity, which he is not very thrilled about. However, unlike the publication of *Rays of*

Light, the publication of "The Pyramid Code" was not in his control, and therefore he could not stop it. At this point, the only thing he can do, which he has already done, is ask that those who may realize his identity not reveal who he is and respect his wishes for remaining anonymous.

INSIGHTS

First and foremost, what is an "insight"? An insight is the capacity to gain an accurate and deep intuitive understanding of something. In other words, it is the ability to truly "see within" something, which is why it is called an "insight." When insights are realized, information that was once simply linear words expressing an idea suddenly becomes a whole lot deeper and can be seen from a completely different angle and understanding. In addition to this, when insights are realized, the interconnectivity among anything and everything becomes significantly more apparent.

For this reason, rather than simply focusing on the information I have received over the past few years, whether through experience, from reading "The Pyramid Code," or from reading portions of *Rays of Light*, I am going to focus on their insights. It is important for me to mention that the following insights in this book are just a portion of what can be extracted and deduced from the information I have received over the past few years. I encourage you to think for yourself and allow yourself to realize other insights, beyond just the ones that are shared throughout this book.

When it comes to "The Pyramid Code" and *Rays of Light*, the insights that I have received and realized may not be apparent to someone reading the documents. My intention in sharing these insights is to guide the reader in reaching a higher level of understanding of the information that has been provided, as well as a higher level of general awareness and consciousness. The following insights, which will be shared in this book, include a wide range of information from both "The Pyramid Code" and *Rays of Light* such as:

1. Understanding the true criteria for life and what "alive" truly means through the knowledge of the power of the pyramids.

2. Understanding the spiritual suppression and enslavement that has been imposed upon the human race through the knowledge of the power of awareness as well as the numerology behind the pyramids.

3. Understanding why extraterrestrials visit us, and in some cases even live among us, through the knowledge of the importance and significance of planet Earth.

4. Understanding the true power of the food we consume, the thoughts that we think, and the words that we speak through the knowledge of how all this affects both our individual and collective levels of awareness and consciousness.

5. Understanding our collective destiny that we will reach unconditionally through the knowledge of fifth-dimensional awareness.

Some of the following information and insights that I am going to bring forth have never been revealed to the public, until now. At this point in time, I invite you to let go of any limitations you may have regarding what you consider to be possible. Some of these insights are derived from information that may sound unbelievable. For example, "The Pyramid Code" suggests that we, the human race, are actually the offspring of the interbreeding between extraterrestrials and humans. The majority of the world may call someone crazy for suggesting such a reality.

However, I want to remind you that the accepted narrative today is that we are the effect of a single-celled organism that eventually evolved into a fish, which eventually grew legs as well as the ability to breathe outside of water, which eventually turned into a full-blown ape and eventually into the modern-day human. However, the basic idea of evolution is survival of the fittest, which implies that if the evolution of the human race truly occurred in this way, then everything that came before us in the line of evolution should have been extinct, yet somehow, this is not the case.

For just a moment, let's try to let go of this belief system and start fresh. Now, what sounds more unbelievable to you? The idea that we are the result of an evolution process in which we used to be fish that has little to no resemblance to our modern-day form (while fish still exist today), or the idea that we are simply the result of the interbreeding between two races that already had physiological features very similar to ours? Have you ever asked yourself how it is possible that we have so much diversity here on Earth? When you merge this idea with abundant evidence of different races coming to Earth thousands of years ago presenting a diverse range of physiological features, is it so far-fetched to suggest that diversity here on Earth is the result of multiple different races interbreeding with mankind?

Simply look at the Egyptian hieroglyphics and you will see that even the Egyptians didn't draw themselves as human beings! They drew themselves as beings who were very tall with elongated skulls, which is in fact what they looked like. The following pictures exhibit the model of an ancient Egyptian elongated skull, along with an actual ancient Egyptian carving in which they drew themselves with elongated skulls.

So, what makes this idea crazier than the current narrative of evolution that suggests we used to be fish? It's simple! The only reason why people are not shocked by the narrative that suggests we used to be fish is because that narrative has been widely accepted on a collective level, and we have therefore become numb to the preposterous and arbitrary story that it is conveying! So, I humbly ask you again to do your best to let go of what you have been taught and to be open to the information you are about to receive. I take absolutely no offense if you don't believe it—all I ask is that you allow yourself to be aware of it.

THE CRITERIA FOR LIFE

Among the many insights that can be derived from "The Pyramid Code" are the true criteria for life and what being "alive" truly means. The moment one understands the true power behind the operational functions and uses of the pyramids is the moment one will understand that there is no opposite to "life." In other words, nothing is actually dead. In order to elaborate further, let me start from the beginning.

According to the information that is contained within "The Pyramid Code," in the year 2750 BC, four different races of extraterrestrial beings came down to Earth from four different planets that were destroyed for reasons that I am not aware of. The extraterrestrials who remained were sent here to assimilate with the native race of mankind, and slowly ruled the land in a positive way—not through suppression and control, but through education and guidance. For the most part, they all looked like ordinary human beings, with minor physiological differences, as is explained in "The Pyramid Code."

All four of these races were very high-vibrational and spiritual beings. One of their main intentions in coming here to Earth, beyond for just the need to find a new home planet, was to elevate and transform the corrupt and materialistic race on Earth into a more spiritual race that would bring peace and quiet, without pressure, fights, or wars—a race that would be preoccupied with the spiritual and not the physical. Although their initial success was overwhelming, they eventually became influenced by the lower-vibrational native beings on Earth.

Instead of being high-vibrational spiritual beings, they suddenly found themselves with tyrannical and cruel rulers who instilled fear throughout the land—a very similar reality to what is happening on Earth today. Due to interbreeding between the high-vibrational and low-vibrational races, the high-vibrational races were diluted over time until eventually they were no more. As we understand it today, their mission failed. However, before the failure of their mission, they constructed an overwhelming number of pyramids all around the planet.

The extraterrestrial races brought with them a different form of technology called electromagnetic pulsation (EMP) and electromagnetic laser pulsation (EMLP). In the language of the extraterrestrials who settled in Egypt and elsewhere in Africa, EMP was called Magen, and EMLP was called Magia. This technology gave them the ability to build massive pyramids. Originally, there were 666,666 pyramids on Earth. (I will explain the significance of this number in the next chapter.) Today we are left with fewer than 100,000 pyramids of different shapes and sizes. Underneath these massive structures (specifically in Egypt) are very large basements that house the tools and technology used to make them.

The Purpose of the Pyramids

The pyramids, when activated, hold the key to understanding the true criteria for life and what "alive" truly means. So, what were the true uses and functions of the pyramids? There is a common belief that the pyramids were used as tombs. Although this is partially true, it is not the whole truth. First and foremost, both spiritual and physical laws hold the foundations for building the pyramids. For this reason, the construction of a pyramid is what connects the spirit world to the material world. In other words, one of the functions of the pyramids was to connect the higher dimensions to the lower dimensions.

In addition to that, the pyramids acted as places of preservation and protection for the high technology that these advanced races possessed. The reason why we find these beings buried in the pyramids is because the divine bodies of these high-vibrational beings were used as energetic defense mechanisms to further ensure the protection and preservation of the high technology that these advanced races stored in the pyramids. The energy that they held within their bodies, even after "death," was intended to act as the gatekeeper and protection for the pyramids, their entrances, and the instruments that exist within them.

Other uses and functions of the pyramids included an eternal clock, an eternal calendar, a lighthouse for both humans and various crafts during the day and at night, a center of connection between man and the divine (God), and spaceships. Yes, the pyramids were used as spaceships. The following is a short excerpt from "The Pyramid Code":

> *Every pyramid can shrink its stone base in order to levitate by contracting the stones and rocks at its base into the pyramid itself.*

> *Every pyramid, regardless of its size or location, can fly to any distance regardless of space or time.*

> *Every pyramid is an independent spaceship, and some have also served as motherships.*

> *Every pyramid moves through the use of magnets in its base, the energy of the sun, and the power of thought of its operators.*

Everything is Alive

So, how were the pyramids able to move as if they were "alive" when activated, if they are built of what we perceive to be inanimate and "dead" stone? Well, is stone really "dead," as most of us have been led to believe? The real question is, does the reality of anything in this universe (whether animate or inanimate) not being "alive" actually exist?

Well, the first question that must be asked is what are the true criteria for what constitutes something being "alive"? Is it possible that the requirements and limitations that we have set to determine whether something is alive or not are tainted by our limitations of awareness and perception?

In order to determine if this is a possibility, let's begin with the scientific requirements and criteria for life. In other words, how is "life" determined according to modern science? According to science, the following criteria must be met in order for something to be considered "alive":

a. Need for energy
b. Organization in membrane-bound cells
c. Genetic information

d. Ability to replicate

e. Growth and response to stimuli

The issue with modern science is that it focuses only on physical and observable phenomena, and it deems anything that cannot be measured by modern scientific instruments as a pseudoscience. As Nikola Tesla once said: "The day science begins to study non-physical phenomena, it will make more progress in one decade than in all the previous centuries of existence." The moment the collective consciousness of modern science decides to make this conscious shift, it will come to realize that the criteria it has set to consider something "alive" are simply a reflection of the collective low level of awareness and consciousness that the human race is currently in resonance with.

The following is a short excerpt from "The Pyramid Code." Please note that the word "God" in this context has no connection to the religious idea of God, but rather to the intelligent, boundless, eternal, omnipotent, ever-present, and divine force that energetically connects all of creation in the universe.

> *"The presence of God exists everywhere and in everything, whether it be human beings, animals, plant life, inanimate objects, and everything in between. For this reason, we must first understand that a pyramid or any other structure is energetically a part of God. In other words, everything, even an inanimate pyramid, is part of the collective spirit of the universe. This means that physical structures are also controlled by the laws of the spirit world. The three-dimensional world is based on the laws of the spirit world, which we cannot exist without. This means that a pyramid is as much of the eternal Divine Being and alive as anything else in the universe."*

So, what is life? Life is the basis of the universe. And what can everything in the universe, whether animate or inanimate, be reduced to? Energy. Therefore, life is energy and energy is life. According to the scientific law of conservation (which is a foundational energetic law of the universe), energy cannot be created or destroyed. So, when we merge the idea that life is energy and energy is life along with the foundational law that energy cannot be created or destroyed, a fundamental question arises: Does death truly exist as a fundamental reality, or is it just a concept that stands for the fundamental reality of life transitioning into a different form of life? Additionally, when we merge the idea that life is energy and energy is life along with the fact that everything in the universe, whether tangible or intangible, can be reduced to energy, then we clearly understand that there is nothing in the universe that is not energetically and, therefore, fundamentally "alive."

Ultimately, what is it that makes something "alive"? In order to understand the answer to such a question, we must begin with asking who and what are you? So, I invite you to look at yourself for a moment. You are living in a physical body. You have a heart. You have a head. You have a brain. However, if your head is *your* head and your heart is *your* heart, then who are *you*? In other words, when we speak about ourselves, we tend to say "my" body, "my" heart, "my" head. The question here is, what represents the "my" that we are always referring to?

If your body was divided into 10 different parts, and each part was put in a geographical location, where are *you*? If you are not your head, your heart, your eyes, your legs, or any other part of your body, then what are you? You are not your job. You are not your money. You are more than just a father, a mother, a sister, or a brother. These are all simply identifications that describe your physical existence—however, *you* transcend all these things! I invite you to let go of these identifications that you confuse for yourself and see what is left.

Whatever makes life possible in the first place is what *you* are. The ability to be aware and conscious, to any capacity whatsoever, is the foundation of what makes life possible. Why? Because without awareness, life could not exist in the first place. This means that the ability to be aware and conscious, to any capacity, is what constitutes if something is "alive," and since everything is energy and energy is consciousness, there is no such thing in the universe that is not "alive." There never has been and there never will be.

Ultimately, life is constituted by something that has some level of awareness or consciousness. After all, everything in the physical world is made of atoms, atoms are made of energy, and energy is made of consciousness. With this idea in mind, a pyramid is no less alive than a human being, because we are both comprised of energy, and therefore we both have some degree of consciousness and awareness, even if it's a level of awareness and consciousness that we don't have the ability to perceive at our current level of awareness. This is the reason why the pyramids were able to move as if they were alive—because they were!

Stone is not dead. Nothing is! They are energetically alive and therefore, have some level of awareness and consciousness. Although we are not yet at a collective level of awareness in which we are able to perceive the consciousness and awareness of inanimate objects such a rocks and stones, there are some individuals who are able to tap into this level of awareness, Ray being one of them.

At this point, I would like to bring very significant and important research to your awareness regarding the true power of quartz crystals that is only now being rediscovered. Did you know that rocks, stones, and crystals that we have been led to believe are "dead" have the ability to store data and memory? Scientists have figured out a way to store 360 terabytes of data on a simple quartz crystal of only 1 inch in diameter and only a few millimeters thick for an indefinite period of time. The fact that a quartz crystal is able to store data and hold a capacity of memory inherently shows that even an inanimate stone is energetically connected to the same field of awareness and consciousness that we are connected to. This field of consciousness is what energetically and spiritually connects everything and every being in the universe, whether tangible or intangible.

Connecting the Spirit World and the Material World

There is a common misunderstanding that the spirit world and the material world are two separate worlds that are not connected to one another. This could not be further from the truth! Although it may not be apparent at our current level of awareness, the spiritual and the physical operate in union with one another. Although they may seem to be separate on the surface, they are in fact one and the same in their core essence of being.

The following is an excerpt from "The Pyramid Code":

> *"Change and evolution in the spiritual world are propagated by different waves, frequencies, and vibrations that are consistent to each form in nature. This energy remains in these abstract forms until it penetrates matter, which results in the changing of matter or the creation of new matter. This process can be achieved through spiritual words or spiritual powers (via waves, frequencies, and vibrations). In other words, flesh is created differently*

from an animal to a human being. A brain is created differently than a human heart. Everything has its own frequency, its own physicality, and its own spirit within it, that affects its waves and vibrations. As spirit transforms itself into physical matter, the material that culminates, such as the death of a body reverses its direction and returns back to spirit. It then further transforms to become (source) energy/power again. This process continues for many years. It is a very slow process that spans millions of years."

My intention in bringing in this excerpt from the document is to show that the spiritual and the physical are two wings that are in fact part of the same bird! In other words, everything and every being, whether animate or inanimate, is energetically connected to the same field of awareness and consciousness. The extraterrestrials who came to Earth thousands of years ago possess a very high level of awareness and consciousness that allowed them to truly understand this fundamental reality. They understood that the pyramids were just as much alive as they were. Moreover, the extraterrestrials possessed this level of understanding and awareness not just conceptually, but through application and experience as well. It is this level of awareness that provided, and still provides, the extraterrestrials the ability to cause their craft to become extensions of their high-vibrational consciousness.

Because their consciousness transcends the limitations of time and space, they were, and still are, able to operate their craft with no regard for the limitations of time and space. This becomes a possibility when one truly understands, not just conceptually but through application, that a craft, along with any other inanimate object, is connected to the same field of consciousness and life that we are!

The Power of Thought

When one is able to access this field of universal interconnectivity, the power of thought is the key component to be able to bring inanimate objects to "life." The power of thought is what connects the spiritual world to the material world. As a matter of fact, the power of thought is what extraterrestrials use to operate their craft today.

The following excerpt is a paraphrased version of a conversation I had with Ray in regard to his firsthand experiences inside multiple extraterrestrial craft:

> *"The inside of an extraterrestrial craft does not look like what many may think. It is not like the inside of a Boeing 747 cockpit with thousands of buttons. Yes, there are touch-screen buttons, but not so many. The craft work through a combination of physical and*

*spiritual technology. The physical technology consists of technology such as electromagnetic pulsation (EMP), electromagnetic laser pulsation (EMLP), magnets, and energy from the sun. When I speak of spiritual technology, I am referring to 'the power of thought.' The only thing in the entire universe that is faster than the speed of light and the speed of sound is **thought**.*

"Inside every craft, there is a sort of dashboard, which is what the operator uses to operate the craft, sometimes without even touching it. This dashboard is what allows for the craft to become an extension of the operator's consciousness by connecting the physical to the spiritual. It looks like some sort of panel made of what looks to me as some type of glass or clear quartz, but I'm not sure what it is made of. To operate the craft, the operator places their hand on this glass-looking panel,

and through the power of thought, operates the craft. There is no steering wheel or gas-like propulsion. It all works through consciousness. In order to operate such a craft, one must possess a very high level of awareness and consciousness. Since the craft becomes an extension of the operator's consciousness, in order to maneuver the craft in ways that transcend the limitations of time and space, the consciousness of the operator must also transcend the limitations of time and space.

"Have you ever wondered how the craft that we have seen in more recent times, such as the ones filmed by Chad Underwood, a Navy pilot, can maneuver in ways and at speed that are completely against the laws of physics as we know them? Well, it is because these craft are extensions of the operator's consciousness, which also transcends the laws of physics as we know them today."

The high level of awareness that extraterrestrials possess is what gave them access to activate the true power of the pyramids. It is this level of awareness that gave them the ability to turn stone structures into spaceships and craft that were extensions of their consciousness. After all, this is how the pyramids worked thousands of years ago, and this is also how extraterrestrial craft work today. Once again, everything is energy, energy is consciousness, and consciousness is life. There is no duality when it comes to the fundamental reality of life. Life is all there ever has been, all there is, and all there ever will be. With this knowledge and understanding, the idea that the opposite of being "alive" cannot exist may be more apparent. Everything is alive! The question is, to what capacity and through what expression?

THE SPIRITUAL SUPPRESSION
OF HUMANITY

We have been indoctrinated to believe that actions such as telepathic communication, levitating the body, healing through touch, telekinesis, and the like are supernatural acts, but are they? Well, what makes something supernatural in the first place? To be deemed supernatural, something must be an action or an event attributed to some force beyond scientific understanding or the laws of nature as we understand them today. In other words, what we consider "natural" is simply a reflection of our current collective level of awareness and understanding. If something is beyond our current level of awareness of understanding, it is considered to be supernatural. Is it possible that what we consider to be supernatural is actually very natural, only we consider it supernatural because our current level of awareness and understanding is being suppressed and is therefore "sub-natural"?

The Supernatural is Actually Natural

Let's take a moment to look at the natural world. When I refer to the natural world, I am not referring to the way we live as human beings, because almost everything we do in modern society is against the laws of nature. I am referring to the parts of nature and the animal kingdom that have not yet been corrupted by humanity. Modern humans need high-tech scientific instruments in order to detect upcoming changes in weather, whereas animals in the natural world are able to detect these changes naturally.

In other words, when a bird can detect a hurricane 500 miles away it is a natural phenomenon, but if a human were able to detect such a thing without the use of scientific instruments, it is considered supernatural. Why? Additionally, humans get an annual sickness on the collective level called the "flu," yet nowhere in nature do we see this as a reality. Cancer and heart disease are the leading causes of death in the human population, killing millions of people, yet these diseases are close to foreign to the natural world.

The question is, do we really live natural lives, or do we live "sub-natural" lives? Why do we consider the ability to see the future or intuitively feel irregularities in one's health to be supernatural? Well, because relative to our current collective level of awareness, these abilities far exceed those of the collective. However, these acts are not supernatural—they are very natural! The key factor we have been missing in this equation is that we don't live according to nature. We are "sub-natural," which makes the natural seem supernatural relative to our current level of awareness and understanding. The root cause for this is the low level of awareness and misguided belief systems with which we are currently and collectively in resonance.

Becoming Aware

In order to reclaim our access to the true power we hold, we must first become aware that this power exists. In other words, you cannot fly without first having the awareness that you have wings! This is why knowledge and awareness are so important. They are the first steps in the journey of understanding and accessing the limitless power that is within us. In order to reach new levels of awareness and understanding, we must first do our best to let go of the limitations that we have been indoctrinated to believe are real.

For example, we are led to believe that levitation and flight with the body is a fantasy that can exist only in the movies, but is this true? Is it really so far-fetched? Before dismissing the idea of levitation and flight with the body as a fantasy, have you ever actually thought about how it might be possible to do? It's quite simple, actually. Levitation and flight with the body become possible when one possesses the knowledge of how to manipulate the force of gravity. In other words, levitation and flight with the body is a result of being able to manipulate energy. So, the question is not "Can you fly?" but "Can you manipulate energy?" That's really what it comes down to. This is why knowledge is power—it gives us the ability to access, through awareness, the true power that we possess.

The Suppression of Knowledge

Knowledge having to do with levitation, telepathic communication, and similar abilities has been hidden from us. This information has been and is being suppressed in order to keep us from accessing our true power. Suppression is nothing new. For centuries, humans have been shamed and sometimes even killed for revealing their true power and their "supernatural" abilities. For example, left-handed individuals, who are right-brain-dominant, have been shamed for centuries.

Did you know that the activation of the right hemisphere of the brain is a key factor in accessing spiritual abilities and our higher power? Yet for many years people were taught that left-handed individuals were "servants of the devil." Teachers would even hit children who wrote with their left hands, in order to stop them so they would learn how to write with their right hands. Have you ever wondered why your right hand is called your "right" hand? The brainwashing is much deeper than we can even comprehend!

Another example is the idea of witchcraft. We have been indoctrinated to believe that anyone who practices witchcraft must be "evil." This indoctrination is not just a relic of the past, but has followed us into modern day as well! Just look at how witches are portrayed in Hollywood movies. This is brainwashing and indoctrination at its finest. In the 1600s, anyone believed to be practicing witchcraft (which is simply the knowledge and ability to manipulate energy) was either burned alive or executed by hanging! Did you know that left-handed individuals were associated with the idea of witchcraft as well?

Measures have been taken to keep us suppressed through physical means as well. For example, our water is filled with chlorine and fluoride, which poison the body and calcify the pineal gland. Our food is filled with chemicals and pesticides, which keep us at a lower vibration of being. The air we breathe is filled with toxins and pollutants, which keep us spiritually numb. And this is not to mention the intense levels of radiation that we face in every aspect of our lives from the technology that our modern society is built on.

The Intention of Suppression

Have you ever wondered why we have been indoctrinated in a way that keeps us disconnected from the true power we hold? Have you ever wondered why information regarding the spiritual foundations of the universe has been censored throughout the centuries? Have you ever wondered why individuals who possessed any sort of "supernatural" abilities were either shamed or executed throughout history? Have you ever wondered why we are being physically poisoned through our food, water, technology, and modern way of life?

Who would intentionally do such a thing, and why would they do it? Why would anybody ever want to hinder us from reaching and realizing the true power that exists within us? The answer to this question exists within humanity's history, as well as what we are experiencing in more modern times. Throughout history, books filled with spiritual insights and truth were burned. The authorities at the time told the people that the information the books contained was dangerous, and that burning them was for the "protection of the people."

Today, we know that was a lie to keep the people suppressed and under the control of both the government and religious leaders at the time. In the year 2020, we experienced a very similar reality with the COVID-19 pandemic. Companies such as Facebook, Instagram, and YouTube have been censoring information and deleting accounts left and right! I've been censored on these platforms multiple times for posting interviews that I have conducted with world-renowned individuals, leaders, and doctors such David Icke, Robert F. Kennedy, Jr., Dr. Christiane Northrup, Dr. Lawrence Palevsky, and many others who shared scientifically backed truths regarding the virus and why it is not being handled in the appropriate way. The censorship is done by what they call "independent fact checkers" who are responsible for labeling anything that is not in alignment with the mainstream narrative as false, with absolutely no scientific backing.

Many times, these "independent fact checkers" base their conclusions on articles written by the mainstream media, which is simply a different wing of the same bird. Whenever I asked why such information was being censored even though it was backed scientifically and conveyed by world-renowned doctors who are more qualified to share medical information than the mainstream media, I was simply told that alternative views are dangerous to society and they must either be deleted or censored in order to "protect the people."

To me, it seems like this is the equivalent of modern-day book burning, only it is done through the censorship and deletion of digital information. History is repeating itself, and because we've been suppressed and kept asleep for so long, the collective agrees with the censorship because they truly believe that it's best for the authorities to make decisions on their behalf regarding the information they should and should not see. We are living in dangerous times! At this point, the answer to why anybody would ever want to hinder us from reaching and realizing the true power that exists within us should be more apparent: power and control. As we've seen throughout history, as well as in more modern times, there have always been a select few who want to control the many.

Targeting Awareness

The genius of the individuals who want to keep humanity under their power and control is that they don't do this only through physical means, but through spiritual means as well. They understand that awareness of knowledge and the truth is what gives us access to our power. In other words, they understand that access to the infinite spiritual power that we possess is directly in alignment with how aware we are. They understand that the higher our level of awareness, the more access we have to our true nature, which is limitless. And therefore, the less aware we are, the easier we are to control.

This is why knowledge has been so deeply censored in the past and is continuing to be censored in the present day—because knowledge gives us higher awareness and higher awareness gives us power! The individuals who want to keep us under their power and control understand that the only way for the few to successfully control billions of people is by targeting us from the source of our power: awareness! After all, if we were aware of the truth, the few would stand no chance against a revolution led by the many. The following is an excerpt from "The Pyramid Code":

"Before the Exodus, there were 666,666 pyramids on Earth. Today we are left with fewer than 100,000 pyramids of different shapes and sizes."

After the publication of "The Pyramid Code," I received questions from people all around the world asking me why the pharaohs of ancient Egypt, who were such high-vibrational beings, associated the pyramids with a satanic and evil number. Well, 666 is not an evil number! On the contrary, the reason why the pharaohs incorporated such a number into their way of life is because they understood its true meaning, which is "life."

In order to understand why this is so, I must first explain the concept on "gematria," which is a concept the extraterrestrials who built the pyramids understood on a very deep level. Please note that although gematria is connected to the Hebrew language, it has absolutely nothing to do with religion. Contrary to common belief, the Hebrew language did not actually originate from the Jewish people. The Jewish people simply adopted the language. Even in Hebrew, the language is not referred to as the "Jewish language," but rather the "holy language." As a matter of fact, letters from the Hebrew alphabet are parts of the actual code to unlock the true power of the pyramids. The Pharaohs of ancient Egypt used and deeply understood the significance of the Hebrew alphabet and gematria.

The Significance of Gematria

Gematria is an alphanumeric code embedded within the Hebrew alphabet, which assigns a numerical value to a word based on the sum of its letters. There are 27 letters in the Hebrew alphabet, which can be converted to numbers ranging from 1 to 900. As shown below, each letter has a numerical value assigned to it, in which it can be converted to:

100	ק	10	י	1	א
200	ר	20	כ	2	ב
300	ש	30	ל	3	ג
400	ת	40	מ	4	ד
500	ך	50	נ	5	ה
600	ם	60	ס	6	ו
700	ן	70	ע	7	ז
800	ף	80	פ	8	ח
900	ץ	90	צ	9	ט

When letters are combined to make words, the letters are added up to give a numerical value to the actual word. For example, the word for "life" in Hebrew is spelled as follows: חי (pronounced "Khai"). The numerical value assigned to the first letter in the word (ח) is 8, and the numerical value assigned to the second letter in the word (י) is 10. When we add these numbers (which are in fact letters) together, we get a value of 18. Therefore, the number 18 represents "life"!

With this understanding, the numerical value of 666 was never considered to be representative of evil in ancient Egypt. On the contrary, 6+6+6=18, which therefore represents life. As a matter of fact, if you spell "evil" backwards, what do you get? L-I-V-E! Additionally, did you know that the general frequency of the human body, as well as Earth as a whole, is 7.83 Hertz? Have you ever tried adding these numbers up? If you do, you will see that they, too, add up to a sum of 18 (7+8+3=18)!

The number 13 is no different. We have been brainwashed to believe that 13 is an unlucky number. The fear of the number is so deeply rooted within our belief systems that even buildings refuse to label the 13th floor as the 13th floor. The truth is, the number represents the frequency of "Love"! How? Well, the Hebrew word for "Love" is "אהבה" (pronounced "ahava"). If you add up the sum of each of the four letters in this word according to gematria, you will see that this word equates to a numerical value of 13 (1+5+2+5=13).

The following excerpt is from "The Pyramid Code." My intention in bringing this excerpt to your awareness is to show you that the deep understanding of gematria and the significance of the frequency of numbers were even applied to the building of the pyramids:

> *Today, the mysticism of the pyramid shape and structure is hidden, but the day will come when the mysticism will be revealed and transparent. It will no longer be hidden. A pyramid basically embodies everything that was, is, and will be. A pyramid is the connection created by man between the physical and the spiritual. Other than the stone, which is visible to the eye, a pyramid is composed of the following base components:*

18 *laser lights symbolizing life (which is represented by the number 18 in Hebrew) and the divine energy.*

10 *internal and external surfaces symbolizing divine physical and spiritual giving (the word "ten" in Hebrew means "to give" and also represents "wealth") between the creation and the Creator. (The numerical value of "10" always represents "1," 1+0=1, which symbolizes **oneness**).*

8 *lines connecting the vertices through which energies flow infinitely between the base and the vertex (the number 8 symbolizes infinity).*

5 *vertices including the apex at the top of the pyramid, which represents the divine connection that is connected to one's own being. The numerical value of "5" represents the letter "ה" in Hebrew, which symbolizes the Divine God.*

The same individuals who have been trying to suppress the human race for millennia for the purposes of power and control have suppressed and censored this knowledge from the mainstream flow of information that is constantly fed to us. They have taken powerful frequencies that are beneficial to humanity, such as the "life" and "love," and disguised them as something that is harmful to humanity so we no longer use it! Isn't that genius? The moment we become aware of the truth behind numbers such as 666 and 13, we will no longer fear them!

After all, there is nothing to be afraid of because they are here to help us shift into a higher consciousness! The time has come for us to take the positive frequencies that have been stolen and hijacked from us in order to keep us suppressed and bring them back into our lives with their true and powerful meanings in our awareness. Remember, the individuals who are trying to keep humanity under their power and control understand that we are energetic and spiritual beings. This is the reason why they have taken certain frequencies (numbers) that are beneficial for humanity's spiritual progression and disguised them as numbers that are harmful.

We have been taught to fear anything that can help us progress spiritually and reach a higher state of awareness and consciousness because if we reached a higher level of awareness and consciousness, these individuals would have less power and control over us. Do you think it is a coincidence that everything having to do with us realizing our true power as spiritual beings is labeled as evil, harmful, or dangerous?

Taking Responsibility

Have you ever asked yourself why our world looks the way it looks today? How did we get to such a point where the truth is being suppressed and censored while the majority of humanity is so asleep that we are not even aware that we are being suppressed? The only reason our world looks the way it looks today is because we, the people, allowed it to look like this. After all, the reality we experience is simply a reflection of our collective consciousness.

An extreme example that I use to get this point across is the existence of Adolf Hitler. From an energetic standpoint, Hitler was not the problem. Hitler was simply a reflection of our consciousness at that time. He existed because the collective allowed it to happen. He was literally democratically elected to power. He was a creation of us, the many! Although we see the few controlling the many, the blame is not in the few because the power is in the many and therefore our reality, no matter what it looks like, is our responsibility.

For us to make a change for the better in this world, we must begin by taking responsibility for our actions.

It's very easy to blame the few who control the many, but we (the many) are forgetting that the few who control the many have not taken our power—rather we have given them our power! We have given the few the right to choose what information should be suppressed and what information should be fed to us. We have given the few the right to think for us, and we therefore have forgotten what it is like to think for ourselves! We have collectively allowed this to happen because most of humanity truly thinks that the few had, and still have, our best interests in mind.

Well, there was a time in distant history when the few did have our best interests in mind—however, that time is no more. The moment we shifted into resonance with vibrations such as evil, corruption, greed, and war is the moment the best interest for humanity was no longer a concern of the few. Ultimately, the many is where the true power resides. The moment we become aware of this truth is the moment we will be able to reclaim our power on the collective level! We, the people, are responsible for the way our world looks today, which means we, the people, have the ability to shift it back into a high vibration that is not in resonance with evil, corruption, greed, and war but with light, peace, unity, and love!

We, the people who hold the true power, must make a shift not through hate, war, or violence, but through light, peace, and love. We must come together and we must unite. We must lose our victim mentality because the world is a reflection of ourselves, which means that when we change ourselves, we change the world. It's time for us to open our eyes. It's time for us to wake up. It's time for us to become more aware and conscious. It's time for us to take our power back peacefully so we can finally live in a world that we deserve to live in—a world of equality, a world of love, and a world of peace.

Don't be afraid to share your truth, even if you are censored for it. The very action of sharing your truth, whether it's censored or not, is a step in the right direction of shifting the collective consciousness through shifting your individual consciousness. After all, we are all individually a part of the collective! I invite you to educate yourself with no limit, and do your best to educate others around you without force or judgment. Together, let's raise our collective vibration, not to one of fear, but to one of love! Together, in unity, we will prevail!

THE IMPORTANCE OF
PLANET EARTH

Physically speaking, Earth is a tiny speck of dust in an infinite and boundless universe. Just look at it in comparison to everything else in the universe. Did you know that 1,300 Earths could fit inside Jupiter? Did you know that 1 million Earths could fit inside the sun? Are you aware that the Milky Way galaxy is 6.7×10^{39} times bigger than Earth? Keep in mind, that is just Earth compared to the tiny little Milky Way galaxy that we happen to be located in.

There are an estimated 170 billion galaxies in the observable universe, which only accounts for what we are able to perceive from our current level of awareness, which is quite limited at the moment. So, why is Earth so important if it is such a tiny planet in this vast and apparently limitless universe?

Why do extraterrestrials, who are physically and spiritually more advanced than we are, bother coming to this planet in the first place? Although Earth may seem to be tiny on the physical plane, energetically Earth is absolutely gigantic! Beyond its energetic significance in the universe, Earth is also quite unique, as it is very different from other planets where life exists.

The Energetic Center of the Universe

Let's begin with the energetic and spiritual importance of Earth. In Jerusalem, there is a structure called the Dome of the Rock, which is a Muslim shrine in modern-day Israel. It is called the Dome of the Rock because the structure is a mosque with a massive gold dome that was constructed directly over what is known as the "Foundation Stone" (although it is more of a massive boulder that the mosque is built around).

The Dome of the Rock   The Foundation Stone

This geographical location is very important to Jewish people as well. This is because this energetically and spiritually rich geographic location on Earth was a big part of their history as a nation. In the year 831 BC, the first holy temple of the Jewish people was built around the same foundation stone where the modern Muslim Mosque is currently built. Although this geographical location was turned into a religiously significant point on Earth, its roots stem from spiritual significance and importance.

The reason why it is called the Foundation Stone is because it is considered to be the place from which the creation of the universe began (not just Earth, but the entire universe).

Although it seems that religion guided the construction of structures in this very location, it was the energetic importance of this geographical location that guided religious leaders to choose this location in the first place. This location—like many geographical locations around the world with ancient structures on them, including the pyramids in Egypt—was chosen by religious leaders for multiple reasons.

First, intersecting ley lines (various supposed alignments of ancient monuments and prehistoric sites in straight lines, believed by some to indicate paths of positive energy inherent in the Earth) exist within this geographical location. As you may know, these make it significantly more powerful in the energetic and spiritual realms.

More important, the exact geographical location of the Foundation Stone is not just the energetic center of planet Earth, but the energetic center of the entire universe, where creation, as we know it, first occurred. As I mentioned, although Earth may seem tiny in the physical realm of experience . . . energetically it is gigantic. This reality is reflected within our planet as well as in the same country that houses the Foundation Stone: Israel.

Although Israel may seem like a little speck of dust on the physical realm of experience, people from all over the world know about it because it is energetically gigantic! I am sure there is limitless mysticism regarding Earth housing the physical energetic center of the Universe, but I am not a mystic. Once again, I am just the messenger. One of the purposes of this book is to share information with the world that I have received from TLS and this is a part of that information.

Extraterrestrial Life

Now that we understand part of the energetic and spiritual importance of Earth, the fact that extraterrestrials come all the way here from extremely far distances may make a little more sense. However, the fact that Earth holds the geographical energetic center of the universe is not the only reason why they have been visiting us, and in some cases even living among us, for so many years.

Before I explain some of these other reasons, it is important to establish an understanding of who some of these extraterrestrials are, how they live, the awareness through which they experience life, and much more.

With the experience, knowledge, and information I have acquired over the past couple of years, I personally know of three extraterrestrial races, including in-depth details. Ray has not only worked with some of these extraterrestrials but he has also been to their planets through his work with TLS.

The intention of sharing this information with you is to provide you with a better understanding of who these extraterrestrials are and how life looks beyond planet Earth. Once you understand this, the importance and uniqueness of Earth in this vast universe should become more apparent. Please note that there are many other races out there, and these are just the ones I know of. Also, none of these planets are in our galaxy, and there is constant communication between TLS and all these races. The names of the planets as I know them are:

1. **Tzia**
2. **Nashia**
3. **Konom**

The people of **Tzia** are most similar in description to the race that is known as the "Pleiadeans," however, I do not know if they are the same race, or just a similar race. As for their physical features, they are Scandinavian-looking, with a slight tan. They are tall and muscular. They have blond hair and green eyes, and they are roughly 7 to 9 feet tall. They also have belly buttons, which gives insight into their birthing process. In regard to their clothing, they wear toga-like garments made of a material that resembles the same fabric a potato sack is made of.

Tzia has three suns and no moon, so it is always daytime there. The climate is very hot (140 to 150 degrees F), which poses many risks for the people, since they experience an immense lack of water. Their lifespan used to be 360 years (according to Earth time), but due to their planetary issues (the water shortage), their average lifespan is currently 180 years. Overall, their population is decreasing due to the water shortage they are experiencing from the planet's very hot climate.

To combat this planetary issue, they take some water from Earth, among other places (which is the explanation for the occasionally mysteriously disappearing lake known as "Lake George" in Australia). However, they depend mainly on ice fields suspended in space for their water. They possess a certain technology that allows them to condense their water to facilitate the process.

Regarding the food they consume, they have only vegetables on their planet. Some vegetables resemble those here on Earth, but most of them we don't recognize. They mostly eat their food raw, however sometimes they do cook their food for medicinal purposes. They use some sort of radioactive material, as opposed to fire, to heat their food when it's used for medicinal purposes. They generally communicate telepathically, however, they do have a physical language as well. Regarding their culture, they are highly sexual beings and they reproduce for pleasure as well. Making love with the same sex is something that is common and accepted in their culture.

The people of **Nashia** are unlike any race I have heard of before. I don't know of any similarities. They are short (roughly 4 feet tall), big-boned, and strong. They don't have noses or ears—they simply have holes in their heads. They have hairy bodies, black hair, black eyes, round heads, round eyes, and round mouths. Like the people of Tzia, they also wear toga-like clothing made up of what looks like a white, cotton-like material. Nashia has two suns and one moon, and nighttime is only two hours long, which is when they sleep. What's interesting is that it only rains when they sleep during those two hours at night.

Their planet is very tropical and wet but there aren't any oceans or lakes. All the water is absorbed into the ground. The landscape is very green. They have only fruits on their planet, and all their fruits are green, which means that they are vegans who consume only raw food, which is a big factor that contributes to their high-vibrational level of awareness. Their lifespan is roughly 13 to 14 years.

Their society is quite interesting as well. They don't have a government or a police force as we do here. They mainly live in communities. Money does not exist in their society or culture. Their work is focused on agriculture, and they have centers of trade. Regarding their reproduction process, they reproduce only to have children and not for pleasure, whereas the people of Tzia reproduce for pleasure as well. To travel within the planet, they levitate (if alone) or go by craft (if in groups). Although they have never visited Earth, they do know about our existence here. However, TLS and others have visited them.

The people of **Konom** are most similar in description to the race known as the "grays," however, they don't hold an ounce of evil in their beings. (Contrary to common belief, there are no evil extraterrestrial races—however, I will elaborate on this shortly.) I do not know if they are the same race as the "grays" or just a similar race.

The beings from Konom are roughly 3 feet tall. They have dolphin-like skin, which is constantly damp, shiny, and slippery. They have round heads and round eyes. Their eyes are on the sides of their heads and move similarly to the eyes of lizards. They do not have body or facial hair. They do not defecate or urinate, since everything is released through their skin. Unlike the people of Nashia and Tzia, the people of Konom do not wear clothing. Their average lifespan is roughly 120 years.

Konom has two suns and one moon, and has six days of light and one day of darkness, which causes them to sleep one day a week. In regard to their food, they eat a mixture of different herbs that grow only on their planet. The herbs have a high liquid content, which is where they get their water from. This mixture of herbs acts as a superfood, which provides them with all they need to survive. They store high-power energy and radiation within their bodies that can be used for healing or as a defense mechanism if necessary.

The Shapeshifters

Contrary to common belief, there is no extraterrestrial race that is evil, according to the information that TLS possesses. Although we have been taught to think "invasion" when we think "UFO," there has never been an alien invasion in all of recorded history where UFOs or extraterrestrials posed a negative threat to the human race. When I share this reality with people, I am usually faced with a common question regarding the existence of the reptilian race. According to my knowledge and experience, there is no "reptilian race" as we know it today. (There are dark forces and energies on Earth today, but they are not "extraterrestrial.")

There are, however, human beings who have the ability to shapeshift into reptiles, but they can shapeshift into other animals and creatures as well. The only form that shapeshifters are not able to shift into is any type of sea creature such as a fish, shark, jellyfish, or shrimp. It is important to understand that shapeshifters are not necessarily of a different race. There are human beings who have the ability to shapeshift due to a genetic predisposition which gives them the ability to shift their form.

Energetically, there are 10 different dimensions that make up the universe. However, shapeshifters are able to access a different dimension, which gives them the ability to shift their form. This dimension is known as "Dimension X." Access to this ability allows them to manipulate energy, which impacts the physical realm in order to change their physical form while retaining their energetic and spiritual consciousness.

There is this idea that all shapeshifters are evil and low-vibrational beings. This is not true. Although there are some shapeshifters who use their powers and abilities to do harm, there are many shapeshifters who use their powers and abilities to do good. As a matter of fact, the woman who is the current head of the New York Chapter of TLS is a shapeshifter.

Since we are already on the topic of shapeshifting, I would like to convey the clear distinction between the two types of shapeshifting that I am aware of: physical shapeshifting and holographic shapeshifting. We've already briefly covered the physical shapeshifting process. Now, let's dive a little deeper. In addition to being born with a specific genetic predisposition giving one the ability to shapeshift, one must also be taught how to access the ability to shapeshift. However, people who are not born with the ability cannot be taught how to do it. Additionally, the process occurs in a fraction of a second, and the individual can hold their form as long as they need to.

Shapeshifters do not take over another being's form, but simply create a "copy" of it on both the physical and the energetic level. Although their form changes throughout the process, their consciousness remains the same. However, they do take on the energy of the being they are forming into, such as accent, language, mannerisms, and so on.

So how does the holographic shapeshifting process differ? In many ways. Unlike the physical shapeshifting process, it takes quite some time to shift through the holographic process (a year in some cases, if not longer). However, once the process is complete, a being can shift back and forth instantaneously. Energetic and holographic memory makes this possible. The holographic shapeshifting process is done through the conscious manipulation of density.

What I find most interesting is that although you can put your hand right through the body of an individual going through the holographic shapeshifting process, clothes still sit on their body, and they can still consume food and drink water without it falling through the body. In order to see the food or water through the body, you would have to be looking at a place where clothes are not covering the body—for example, the throat. There are many races who have this ability to shift holographically. Human beings can do this as well, through specific training and by learning certain energetic formulas and codes.

At this point, you may be asking, "How are all of these abilities even used? For what purpose?" Before moving back to the topic of extraterrestrials, I feel it is important to briefly answer this question. Shapeshifting be can applied in many different ways.

For example, a shapeshifter can turn into another agent in TLS in order to cover for them. In other words, a shapeshifter could be sitting at dinner with the agent's family, undercover as the agent, while that agent is on a mission. That's something that has happened with Ray quite a few times!

Another example could be an extraterrestrial shifting into human form for the primary purposes of learning and studying the human race in order to assimilate, with the intention of eventually reaching a state of intergalactic unity.

Earth is Unique

Now that we've covered the basics of who these extraterrestrials are and how they live, the next question is: What makes planet Earth so unique? Well, for starters, animals don't exist anywhere except on Earth. This means that on top of the fact that we are the only race who has domesticated pets such as cats and dogs, we are also the only race that consumes animal products (which are low-vibrational "foods" that negatively affect our level of awareness and consciousness). There are some planets where the inhabitants live primarily off of sun radiation, moon radiation, water (different than the composition of Earth water as we know it), herbs, or in some cases just soil.

Additionally, we are the only race that is bound to the limitations of time and space, which is a direct reflection of our low level of awareness and consciousness. Earth is the only planet with war and disease. Due to the high level of awareness that extraterrestrial beings are in resonance with, war and disease are foreign concepts to these races. They either experience natural death, such as in their sleep, or accidental death, such as a physical accident.

They don't experience disease because they live according to the land, and their way of life is directed and guided by their higher level of awareness and understanding, which does not resonate with disease ("dis-ease"). They don't experience war because war is not something that exists in their level of awareness, which therefore creates their experience of life. War implies that one believes in the illusion of division. They are not bound by such an illusion. War does not exist on their planets because they are truly in resonance with the fact the "we are all *one*." And they truly understand that hurting someone else is the equivalent of hurting themselves. For this reason, war and evil are foreign concepts to these high-vibrational beings.

The following is a direct quote from Ray, who has been to these planets and has worked with these extraterrestrials firsthand:

> *"War exists nowhere else in the universe. Once we get rid of the dark forces here on Earth, the wars on our world will come to an end. Wars*

are being perpetrated by these evil powers. When they are no longer here, everything will change. The awareness that we are lacking is because we are being suppressed by the evil powers that exist. That's why we have greed, corruption, wars, army, police, etc. All of this will disappear once these evil powers disappear and people are no longer suppressed (which is what is referred to as the Age of Love). This time will come sooner rather than later."

Extraterrestrial Awareness and Intentions

So, if Earth is such a toxic place compared to other planets, why would these physically and spiritually advanced races even bother coming to Earth in the first place? Contrary to common understanding, the fact that Earth is such a toxic place compared to other planets is the very reason why they are here in the first place! We must first understand that the intentions of extraterrestrials have been portrayed falsely for quite some time. Hollywood has brainwashed us to think that extraterrestrials are here to invade us and threaten our existence. This couldn't be further from the truth!

It's time we change that false narrative that the media has created, and shed light on the true intentions of these high-vibrational beings. First and foremost, the level of awareness and consciousness these extraterrestrials possess must be acknowledged! They possess an extremely high level of awareness and consciousness and therefore, experience a very high-vibrational reality of life. This high level of awareness allows them to break through the illusions of not just time and space, but also division and separation. They don't just "understand" the idea of "we are all one"—they live in complete resonance with that fundamental reality.

They understand completely that there is no difference between us and them. There is no "you" and "I" in their high level of understanding. The only concept they understand is "we," which is the true and fundamental reality that exists energetically. The only reason that we are even capable of thinking that they are here to invade us is because we experience life in resonance with frequencies such as fear, greed, corruption, and war. We are suppressed and believe false realities, whereas they are liberated and see through the illusions that we live by.

Here on Earth, we live according to the illusion of division and separation. We live according to the concept of "us" and "them," as well as the concept of "you" and "I." Just look at the world around you and you will see this reflected in every aspect of our lives. We have countries that are separated by borders. These borders are not real—they are simply illusionary lines that we, the human race, have created and accepted as divisions between land that is interconnected in every way, shape, and form.

This level of awareness leads us to care only about what is going on in "our" country instead of "our" planet or "our" universe. It's this level of awareness that makes it complicated to understand why extraterrestrials would come to such a toxic place in the first place. Why? Because in our current collective level of awareness, we think only about ourselves, without the understanding that we are all one. The first thing most human beings feel when someone goes out of their way to do something positive is suspicion, and there is always the question of "what's in it for them?" This is a direct reflection of our low-vibrational collective consciousness.

When I asked Ray, who has experienced these extraterrestrials and worked with them firsthand, why they would even bother coming to Earth if it is such a toxic place compared to their home planets, he responded as follows:

> *"Cells in the human body are extremely small when compared to the size of the body. However, if there were a single cell in your body that had turned cancerous, and you did nothing about it, eventually that single cell would multiply. And what started as a simple cell that was infinitesimally smaller than the human body would grow to a point where it threatens the survival of the entire body. Toxicity and corruption is the ultimate and most infectious disease."*

This idea sums up a major factor of why extraterrestrials bother coming to Earth in the first place. They understand that what happens on Earth ultimately affects the entire universe. They understand that Earth is not "separate" or "isolated" from their planets because everything is connected and therefore, everything affects everything. When the interconnectivity of everything in this universe is disregarded, the existence of the everything as it is can easily become threatened, which is what is happening today.

This is why extraterrestrials are among us. This is why UFO and extraterrestrial sightings have drastically increased since the use and threat of nuclear weapons began on Earth. The fact that UFOs have been sighted near nuclear facilities while these nuclear facilities were suddenly and mysteriously disarmed is no coincidence! The ultimate goal is to reach the Age of Love and the extraterrestrials understand that although they may have collectively reached fifth- dimensional awareness or higher, "we" as a collective of life in the universe have not reached fifth-dimensional awareness.

In order to reach our collective destiny (and when I say "our," I am referring to all life in the universe), we must do so together, no matter how close or far apart we may be from one another. Extraterrestrials are here to help guide us in order to reach a higher level of awareness here on Earth so we can all reach our collective destiny in this universe once and for all.

A New World Order

At this point, I would like to bring in an important message with insights I have received over the past couple of years that may help others dissolve certain internal limitations and thus allow us, as one, to shift to a higher level of awareness and reach our destiny. The idea of new world order and one-world government is one that triggers and scares many of us, as it should. However, there is a very big factor that we are missing when it comes to these topics. Yes, at our current level of collective awareness, new world order and one-world government would be horrible for the ascension of humanity. This is because if we were to create such a governmental structure while remaining in the collective vibrations of fear, control, and suppression, we would have a very big problem, and the ascension of the human race would indeed be threatened.

However, when we collectively reach fifth-dimensional awareness where fear, control, suppression, evil, and corruption do not exist, one-world government is what we are going to have, and it will no longer be a regression or threat to the human race, but a progression and advancement of the human race. Just look at how the extraterrestrials in Tzia, Nashia, and Konom live! They are unified. They don't have different countries with barriers to entry such as citizenship because they are not citizens of their communities—they are citizens of their planets and furthermore, they are beings of the universe!

Crime, corruption, and evil do not exist in their world because they are not in resonance with such realities. They don't have laws telling them not to kill, murder, rape, or steal because these actions are foreign to them. There is a common misconception that evil, corruption, and greed are simply "part of human nature" and will never go away. This is not true. None of these actions is a part of human nature." These actions and ways of life are simply a part of third-dimensional awareness or lower. As our awareness changes, so will our world! That's where the key to ascension exists. There will come a time when we, the human race, understand that we are all one. More importantly, we won't just conceptualize it, but we will truly live it!

So, what is the ultimate significance of Earth, and why is it especially important at this moment in time? Beyond the fact that Earth houses the physical energetic center of the universe where creation (as we know it) first occurred, Earth is unique in an infinite number of ways. Beyond all that, Earth needs help!

The human race is spiritually and energetically barbaric. We, the human race, are drastically lacking in our collective level of awareness, and we need assistance and guidance in order to break free of the spiritual and energetic imprisonment that we have imposed upon ourselves. We are experiencing a new age of information and assistance like never before. Earth's significance and importance lie in the fact that, in the modern day, Earth holds the potential to destroy the universe while it simultaneously holds the potential to bring all life in the universe into a new era: the Age of Love.

We are living in very important times, times when the human race and the animal kingdom may experience certain events that will change the course of all life in the universe forever. The question is, in what direction? The power to make that choice lies in our hands. As I said earlier, although Earth may seem like just a tiny speck of dust in an infinite and endless universe, its unique characteristics, along with its energetic significance in this endless universe, is what makes it so powerful!

RAISING THE COLLECTIVE VIBRATION

The reality we experience is a reflection of the vibrations with which we are in resonance. Today, we are in resonance with lower vibrations such as evil, corruption, greed, war, division, and so on. However, we have the ability to shift our experience of reality into a much higher state of vibration where the expressions of low-vibrational energy (evil, corruption, greed, war, division, and so on) will become obsolete. Ultimately, our collective level of awareness and consciousness is what dictates our resonance, and our resonance is what dictates our collective experience of reality. This means that in order to shift our collective experience of reality to a reality where the expression of low-vibrational energy is nonexistent, we must first shift our level of awareness and consciousness into a higher state.

With this idea in mind, many of us focus on shifting the collective level of awareness and consciousness because the collective resonance is what ultimately dictates the expression of reality that we experience. However, we tend to forget that in order to raise the collective vibration, we must begin on the level of the individual. This is because each one of us, individually, makes up the collective vibration in the first place. For this reason, we must first focus on raising our individual vibration of being in order to succeed in shifting the collective vibration of being.

The foundation of raising your individual vibration and level of awareness begins with the awareness and true understanding that the body is the root that influences all the dimensions above it, such as the mind, spirit, and soul. In order to reach higher states of awareness, the body must first be pure. In *Rays of Light*, Rabbi AA says the following:

> *"The body is the root that influences the layers that are above it. In the event that the body is ready and pure, it will elevate, and if the body is faulty and corrupt, all the spiritual abundance will be sealed, blocked, hidden, and buried. This is the difference between light and darkness. There is no wholeness for the soul without the body—a healthy body."*

In other words, in order to attain a high level of awareness, a healthy soul may only reside in a healthy body. This means that one must be spiritually healthy—and in order to be spiritually healthy, one must first be physically healthy. This means that, contrary to popular belief, spiritual ascension begins with the state of the physical body.

The purpose of this chapter is to provide knowledge of the effects that foods, thoughts, words, and actions have on one's individual vibration of being. In order to do so, I provide some excerpts from both "The Pyramid Code," along with never-before-seen excerpts from *Rays of Light*. In regard to the excerpts you will read from *Rays of Light*, some excerpts are documentations of dialogues between Rabbi AA and Ray, while other excerpts are lessons and teachings from Rabbi AA that Ray documented as Rabbi AA spoke them.

My intention in bringing these excerpts forth is to convey important teachings, lessons, and mysticism that may help one understand, through application, how to raise one's individual vibration of being. Upon reading some of these excerpts, you will see that many of the teachings are expressed through certain events connected to the history of the Jewish people. Please understand that this is *not* a religious text or a religious teaching whatsoever. These excerpts simply use specific experiences through the lens and language of an individual to express universal insights that apply to all beings, regardless of religion, race, ethnicity, or gender.

My suggestion is to try to let go of the story and read between the lines to understand the insights being expressed. There is one excerpt that mentions the significance of the Torah (the Old Testament). It is important to understand that although in modern times the Torah is associated with religion, it is not a religious book but rather a spiritual and historic book. Unfortunately, it has been corrupted by modern-day religious leaders. The Torah has a code by which it was written, and this code holds the electromagnetic and vibrational "sustenance" for the spirit and the soul, which I explain later on in this chapter.

Please note that the Torah is *not* the only book with divine and universal codes. As I've already mentioned, the information provided here is being given through the lens and experience of an individual. However, there are universal insights within this information that apply to all beings and all nations!

The Power of Food

The food we eat is extremely important when it comes to raising our individual vibration and level of awareness. The pharaohs of ancient Egypt possessed an in-depth understanding regarding the importance of food and the significant impact it has on one's individual vibration of being. Although it is their high level of awareness that allowed them to access such limitless potential and power, the foundation of their high level of awareness and spiritual accessibility existed within the food they consumed. The following is an excerpt from "The Pyramid Code" regarding the food of the Pharaohs:

"There was a continuous connection between the spirit world and the human spirit.

*The early pharaohs were completely vegan—
however, as time went by, they were influenced
by humans, who corrupted their minds, souls,
and bodies through the use of forbidden foods
and forbidden actions. Instead of interacting
with animals, they started eating them. Even the
lions of the royal palace were naturally vegans."*

Unfortunately, the current collective low level of awareness of humanity has resulted in most of humanity forgetting the importance of food when it comes to reaching higher states of consciousness. We are currently suffering from a collective low level of awareness, which has resulted in us consuming vibrationally suppressive poisons and forbidden foods such as gluten, dairy, dead flesh, and processed foods. And we don't even understand why these poisons are poisons to begin with.

In addition to this, most of our "food" is laced with chemicals, which further add to the spiritual suppression of humanity. If you are one of the many who do not understand why consuming these products is not natural, simply look at nature. With the exception of domesticated animals, are there any other animals on this planet that eat food that has been processed? No, so why do we? Are there any other animals on this planet who drink milk from a different species of animal, let alone drink milk past their own mother's maturation of breast feeding? No, so why do we? Are there any other animals on this planet that need to cook their dead flesh, let alone their food, before consuming it? No, so why do we?

The only reason we cook dead flesh in the first place is because we would get sick if we ate it raw. Logically, doesn't that mean we shouldn't be consuming it in the first place? We take part in these absurdities and see nothing wrong with them. Why? Well, because knowledge having to do with spiritual ascension has been hidden from us, and therefore our level of awareness has diminished. This lack of awareness and suppression of knowledge have led us to live lives of decreased physical health, and therefore lives in which many spiritual capabilities are blocked.

Purifying and Preparing the Body

Although many of us think that spiritual acts such as meditation and prayer are the keys to reaching higher states of awareness, these acts will not allow us to reach such heights without first purifying ourselves on the level of the physical and material body through the food that we consume. In other words, food is the sustenance of the body, responsible for keeping the body healthy and alive, and therefore, it is the foundational tool that must be used in order to prepare the body to attain a higher vibration of being and receive spiritual abundance.

The following is a short excerpt from *Rays of Light*. It is the documentation of an important dialogue between Ray and Rabbi AA, which covers the significance of the consumption of food in connection with receiving spiritual abundance:

> **Rabbi AA:** *Allow me to try and summarize very briefly what we have learned together in recent months in order to advance you in the healing of your body and your mind. As always, do not forget that all of what you have written thus far, are writing now, and will write in the future does not only relate to you, but to the entire world and all of its dimensions. I would like to take you back to the year 2408* (This is 1353 BCE, according to the Gregorian calendar.)

> **Ray:** *You mean 2448?* (This is 1312 BCE according to the Gregorian calendar.)

> **Rabbi AA:** *No. 2408. In the year 2408 (1353 BC), the Hebrews received manna*

from the sky. For a period of 40 years, they ate the manna, which is actually a type of bread.

Ray: *I thought manna was a kind of bird, such as quail.*

Rabbi AA: *There are different opinions, but rest assured it was bread. However, it was not ordinary bread. This bread gave the Hebrews spiritual strength and spirit in order to prepare them to receive the Torah (Bible) on Mount Sinai. Here, we must understand that if we were asked what would prepare us for spiritual abundance, we would immediately think of spiritual preparation such as studying, nonstop learning, purity of heart, immersion in ritual baths, prayer, meditation, fasting, and the purification of the soul. We would assume that in order for one to receive such a high-vibrational book, one must transcend the dimension of matter and prepare the body,* *mind, spirit, and soul for supreme spiritual abundance. However, we see the exact opposite. The bread (manna), which is the food/ sustenance of the physical and material body, is what prepared the Hebrews (bodies and souls) for receiving such high-vibrational light . . . There is a deep foundation here: The fact that the principle of the preparation towards spiritual abundance is in the existence of the instruments which belong to the body and takes place with physical eating . . . Manna and Matzah* (the unleavened flatbread in Jewish cuisine, which is the element of the Passover festival) *are the foods of the body, and they help prepare our instrument* (body) *to be able to receive the divine light.*

Ray: *Where are we supposed to get manna from today?* (Ray is asking this question with the intention of finding a way to prepare the body to receive spiritual abundance.)

Rabbi AA: *There are other ways and tools. For example, dew.* (They are referring to the seemingly tiny drops of water that form on cool surfaces at night, when atmospheric water vapor condenses.)

Ray: *Dew?*

Rabbi AA: *Yes, dew. Dew is a spiritual abundance that comes to us every day without any grasp or hold to the land, the Earth, and its layers. The dew gives spiritual abundance and cleanses its surroundings and gives physical matter to us and to our food. As you have already learned, dew represents the 39 spheres of purity.*

So, how and why does the preparation of receiving spiritual abundance exist within physical food? How can something physical lead us to spiritual abundance? In order to understand the answer to this, we must understand the significance of food and why it is so essential to maintain the health and vitality of the human body. The following is an excerpt from *Rays of Light*, in which Rabbi AA teaches Ray about the connection of physical food to the divine light (God):

> *"We must understand that the human being lives and survives from the power of the divine light. The human being's need for food (sustenance) is derived from the fact that the human being does not live from themselves, but rather from God, the source of life. The human being must always be connected to the source of life and be nourished from the abundance of its existence, which is the root cause of why the subject of eating is so important. The human being is composed of four different planes (levels): the soul, the spirit, the mind, and the body. Each one of these levels is in need of sustenance in order to exist, just like*

our physical bodies are in need of food in order to live. Every level is in need of abundance and vitality from its own form of sustenance that it requires. Indeed, the body cannot be nourished by the sustenance of the soul, and the soul cannot be nourished by the sustenance of the body. Here we must learn the secret of the sustenance and abundance. The divine light (God) comes down to all dimensions (the soul, the spirit, the mind and the body) through the nourishment of each one according to its required sustenance. The soul is nourished by the understanding of the secrets and mysticism of the Torah (Bible). The spirit is nourished from the revelations of the Torah (Bible). The mind is nourished from the actions of good deeds. The biggest and most important principles regarding good deeds is for the person who is doing/fulfilling the good deeds to do it with the enthusiasm of the heart and complete happiness with internal desire and huge enthusiasm, and not as if one imposed on him a heavy burden. However, the body must also be nourished from the abundance of the divine light (God). The question that remains is, what is the source of sustenance that nourishes the body? We see that the body is nourished from the physical sustenance of solid or liquid food. We are under the impression that this form of physical sustenance is not nourishment from the abundance of the divine light, but rather from physical foods.

At this point, it is important for me to reiterate that the Torah is not a religious book, but rather a spiritual and historical book. The reason why the secrets, mysticism, and revelations of the Torah are the sustenance for the spirit and soul (as Rabbi AA stated in *Rays of Light*) is because the Torah has a code by which it was written, and the code holds the electromagnetic and vibrational sustenance for these higher dimensions of our being.

The sustenance of the higher dimensions of being (spirit and soul) is electromagnetic frequency (EMF), electromagnetic vibration (EMV), electromagnetic radiation (EMR), electromagnetic light (EML), and electromagnetic oxygen (EMO). The code of the Torah gives one access to the universal understanding of all these frequencies and energies. Once again, there are other books that are not connected to Judaism with divine and universal codes, which hold these same high-vibrational frequencies that act as the sustenance for the spirit and the soul.

My intention in bringing forth the excerpt above is to show that food—although we see and experience it as a physical phenomenon—is one of the tools given to us to help us connect to the divine light from the base of our beings, because it comes from the divine light. As Rabbi AA says in *Rays of Light*: "For every physical creation, there is a higher spiritual root." Eating high-vibrational food is the first step that must be taken, even before acts like meditation and learning, in order to reach a higher level of awareness and consciousness. As we have learned, this is because the body must be elevated and prepared so it can fulfill its function of being an instrument to receive the divine light.

Ultimately, food is the tool that is used to prepare the body for its destiny, and therefore, it is food and the action of eating that will help us prepare ourselves on all levels in order to receive spiritual abundance from the divine light (God). As Rabbi AA states in *Rays of Light*:

> *"We will discover that if we would like to bring the light into the physical world, we need physical instruments made from this world. The divine light (God) is not revealed without the proper tools and instruments to receive it. In order to receive blessings and spiritual abundance, we must be prepared not only with our thoughts and willpower,*

but also in our physical body. This was the role that manna played before the Hebrew received the Torah at Mount Sinai.

The Criteria for High-Vibrational Food

For something to be considered a high-vibrational food, it must have a direct connection to the divine light. This leaves us with foods that get their energy solely from the sun and the rain, such as fruits, vegetables, herbs, and nuts. In *Rays of Light*, Rabbi AA gives guidance on the criteria for choosing foods that contain spiritual abundance. Please note that the rabbi refers to high-vibrational and divine light as "divine sparks" in the following excerpt. The rabbi says the following:

> *"Each and every food, whether forbidden or allowed, possesses a specific energy. Here, we must emphasize the difference between food and between creations that are not food. All*

creations that turn into food (fruits, vegetables, herbs, etc.) are more spiritually rooted than creations which are not food for humans such as rocks, stones, metals, trees, animals, and the like. The secret of sustenance within the food itself is the multiplicity of the divine spark, which exists within the food itself. The human being can only be nourished from the divine light, and we'll find that there is no nourishment from physical food unless divine sparks reside within, which is the root of the food. From this, we shall learn and understand that creations that lack taste and smell lack divine sparks. The nutritious foods that contain spiritual abundance (since they received their life only from the sun and the rain, which is their honorable source) possess good taste, good smell, and they are pleasant to the eye. These foods possess the highest level of divine sparks within them and therefore the highest levels of nourishment and spiritual abundance."

You Are What You Eat

Simply put, food is energy expressed in physical and edible form. Additionally, every food has its own frequency, and therefore, whatever you consume, you energetically and vibrationally become. In *Rays of Light*, Rabbi AA explicitly says, *"The body is built through its nourishment/food. The food that is eaten is digested and becomes part of the human body by means of the replacement of matter* (this is how the body renews itself). *In fact, the human body is comprised of the food that the human eats. Food is the body."* In other words, if you eat low-vibrational foods, you will become that frequency and remain in a state of suppressed awareness where spiritual abundance is blocked.

On the other hand, if you eat high-vibrational foods, you will reach new levels of awareness and consciousness that are in resonance with the food you are consuming. There are indications of this truth all around us at all times. For example, over the past few years, the world has been shifting into a more conscious state than ever before, on the collective level. A big part of this shift is attributed to a change in the food that we collectively consume from low-vibrational and forbidden foods (meat, dairy, and processed foods) to high-vibrational foods (plant-based foods such as raw fruits and vegetables). In *Rays of Light*, Rabbi AA says, "*The human being is destined to eat food of only the highest source, such as plants and vegetables, since these are pure foods which receive their food from the sun and the rain.*"

The reason our consciousness has been shifting into a higher and more spiritual state on the collective level is because these foods hold a higher vibrational resonance, thus causing us to inherit a higher level of awareness on the collective level. Ultimately, these foods are more spiritually rooted and connected to the divine light, and they therefore give us more access to these higher dimensions of reality. For this reason, food is an incredible tool to help us reach the spiritual heights that we strive for—however, it can be detrimental if not used correctly.

The next time you have to choose between a high-vibrational food such as an apple and a forbidden food such as French fries, remember that you are what you eat! Ask yourself which vibration you would prefer to become—the vibration of the deep-fried potato covered in unstructured and poisonous oil, or the vibration of the apple that grew from the Earth and was created with sunlight, water, and universal intelligence. The choice is yours. However, it is important to note that there are cases in which forbidden foods are necessary in order to heal the body if it is sick.

The following excerpt from *Rays of Light*, in which Rabbi AA is speaking to Ray about the use of forbidden foods, teaches us just this:

"Certainly, in the event that a human being or animal becomes ill, the consumption and use of forbidden foods as medicine to heal is allowed. Seemingly, we use filth to get rid of filth from our bodies. For example, when your wife became ill, she needed to drink snake soup. When you injured your body, I directed you to eat animal flesh such as buffalo. As you know, many medicines are made from forbidden foods such as pig. You personally used it on your own body to remedy an illness that you had. However, a human being or animal cannot eat medicinal herbs on a regular basis, such as garlic, unless they are ill. The allowed is forbidden, and the forbidden is allowed, depending upon your state of health. Of course, if we follow the perfect laws of creation and nature and we don't consume the forbidden foods in the first place, then we won't ever need to use forbidden foods to help us heal."

Remember, the first step to reaching spiritual health is maintaining physical health. For this reason, the obsolescence of forbidden foods in your life, along with the reconnection to real and high-vibrational whole foods, is of the utmost importance! As Rabbi AA says to Ray in Rays of Light, "*You already know that forbidden foods truly confuse and contaminate the heart and disrupt a person's ability to receive higher spiritual abundance. When the heart gets confused and contaminated, the divine light does not find its way down to the human body, and illness falls upon us.*" As you eat cleaner, you will vibrate higher. As you vibrate higher, you will become more aware. As you become more aware, you will shift into a much higher vibration of being, which in turn will positively impact your individual level of awareness and therefore positively impact the collective consciousness of humanity! For more information on specific foods to eat, along with their physical and spiritual benefits, I highly recommend you read *Life-Changing Foods* by Anthony William.

Measuring Your Vibration

Since each food has its own vibration, and the vibration of each food is what we become when we consume it, food can also act as a great tool that can be used to indicate and measure your current individual vibration of being. It all comes down to how a specific food makes you feel. Let's use a low-vibrational and forbidden food to show how this works: a cheeseburger!

Because a cheeseburger is a concoction of processed food, dairy, gluten, and dead flesh laced with chemicals, it may be apparent that this food holds a very low vibration. In order to use this food as an indicative tool to measure where you stand vibrationally, you must pay attention to its effect on your body when you consume it. The feeling you have when you consume it will clearly show you whether you are below or above the vibration of it. In other words, if the cheeseburger makes you feel good, that is an indication that you are either below resonance or in resonance with the vibration of the cheeseburger. On the other hand, if the cheeseburger makes you feel sick, this is an indication that your vibration of being is above that of the cheeseburger. This indicative process applies to everything you consume, unless you have a specific food allergy— however, that is a whole different conversation.

I realized this energetic truth through the shift I have made over time in regard to my past consumption of alcohol. When I used to go out to dance with friends, I would drink just like everyone else who went out, and it would make me feel great! Over time, as my consciousness shifted and my vibration increased, alcohol became less and less tempting for me because it started energetically bringing me down instead of lifting me up. Soon after, I came to a clear realization that, in the past, my vibration was relatively lower than the vibration of the alcohol, and therefore, when I consumed it, it made me feel "high." Now that I hold a vibration that is higher relative to the vibration of the alcohol, even the smallest sip makes me sick. This is because I have transcended the vibration of alcohol and therefore, it no longer brings me up, but rather pulls me down.

Food is Your Medicine and Color is Your Guide

In addition to the fact that food can be used as a tool to measure your current individual vibration of being, it can also be used as a tool to heal the body, thus allowing you to reach a higher level of awareness. One of the secrets of learning how to use food as a tool to heal the body lies in the foundational understanding of the connection between the color of a food and the seven major energetic centers (chakras) in the physical body. In order to understand this connection, we must first understand the fact that color is frequency.

The only thing that makes one color different than another color is a differentiation in frequency (vibration). Have you ever wondered why each of the seven chakra points in the human body is represented by a different color? The reason for this is that each color represents a different frequency and therefore, represents the optimal vibration of each part of the body, respectively. In other worlds, the color of each food connects to its bodily function.

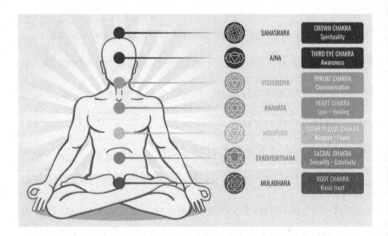

The following excerpt is from my book entitled *Forming the Formless*, in which I included an in-depth explanation regarding how to use color as a guide to choosing the right foods to heal any imbalances in the body and, therefore, to be more physically prepared on the level of the body to receive spiritual abundance:

> *"The human body is a community of different frequencies. There is a map of the human body that has existed for thousands of years. It breaks the human body down to seven major energy centers called chakras. Each chakra is associated with a different part of the body. Each chakra is also associated with a different color based on the frequency that part of your body operates on. Your body is a map of color. Color affects your emotions and your thoughts. It can even tell you what foods are necessary at a specific point in time to physically and energetically rebalance yourself. Additionally, when I refer to food, I am referring to natural food that has not been created or altered by man. Ultimately, food is your medicine, and color is your guide.*

"**Red** vibrates at the same frequency of emotions such as hunger, anger, stress, and aggression. It is the most important chakra to keep balanced because it is the foundation of all your higher chakras. On the physical realm, red corresponds to your hips and specifically your legs, which connect your body to the earth. It is the color that connects you closer to the physical realm rather than the spiritual realm. It is a grounding color. An imbalance of your red chakra can cause bowel disorders, urinary problems, and many other muscular issues associated with the hips and legs. If you are experiencing such issues, simply eat foods that are red: tomatoes, strawberries, and red apples. By surrounding yourself and consuming the frequencies of earth matter that correlate to the red frequency, you, in turn, will inherit that frequency and rebalance your imbalance.

"**Orange** vibrates at the same frequency of feelings such as creativity, ambition, *sexual energy, and addictive behavior. It is a color filled with passion and emotional expression. On the physical realm, orange corresponds to the reproductive organs. If you are experiencing a lack of sexual energy, start surrounding yourself with orange frequencies. Eat carrots and oranges. These foods will surely rebalance your sexual energy to a healthy state.*

*"**Yellow** vibrates at the same frequency of emotions such as positivity, power, inspiration, and intelligence. On the physical realm, yellow corresponds to the spleen and the stomach. It relates directly to digestion. If you suffer from depression or even poor digestion, start spending more time outside in the yellow sun. Eat a mango. Eat a banana. Eat a pineapple. You will soon see that your depression will dissipate as you inherit healthy forms of the yellow frequency from the natural world.*

"**Green** vibrates at the same frequency of feelings such as love, compassion, healing, and giving. On the physical level, green corresponds to your heart and lungs. If you are going through a heartbreak, surround yourself with green. Walk around a luscious garden. Eat a kiwi or a green apple. Embrace and inherit a balanced green frequency.

"**Blue** vibrates at the same frequency of feelings such as communication, truth, and balance. On the physical realm, blue corresponds to your throat and your thyroid. If you experience trouble expressing yourself, spend more time sitting by the ocean. Eat blueberries. Visualize a clear blue sky in your mind's eye, and allow the healthy frequencies of blue to rebalance your system.

"**Indigo** vibrates at the same frequency of feelings such as deep thought, intuition, *and sensitivity. On the physical realm, indigo corresponds to the pituitary gland. If you are trying to focus or attain a higher level of intuition, eat indigo foods, such as blackberries or plums. Visualize the color in your mind, and see how it affects you.*

*"**Violet** vibrates at the same frequency of feeling such as high spiritual attainment and self-actualization. On the physical realm, violet corresponds to the pineal gland. If you are in search of attaining a higher level of spirituality, consume foods such as beets and figs. Doing so will allow you to inherit the highest frequencies in the spectrum of vibration."*

In addition to using the color of food as guidance on what to consume, the shape of the food is equally as important! The shape of a food is generally indicative of what part of the body it can heal. For example, a walnut looks like a brain, and it is also good for the brain. A carrot is good for the eyes and, when you bite into it, it looks like an eye. The list goes on and on. Now that you are aware of how color and shape can be used to further utilize food as a beneficial tool, feel free to use this awareness to raise your vibration of being and, therefore, your level of awareness and consciousness.

The more you learn about the energetic map of the body, along with which color and shape corresponds to each part of the body, the more intuitive eating healthy will be. Once this awareness is fully acquired, the days of being at the mercy of what one doctor or study says over another will be no more. Opinions change, but frequencies do not!

The Power of Thought and Speech

Thought is the link that connects the intangible spirit world and the tangible material world. After all, every tangible action started as an intangible thought! Ultimately, speech is the tool used to express thought through the medium of frequency and vibrations, which we refer to as sound. In *Rays of Light*, Rabbi AA explains to Ray, "*Speech is the instrument used to express thought. Without speech, the person would not be able to express their thoughts. There is no significance to speech without thought, and there is no significance to thought without speech (the instrument/tool which materializes the expression).*"

What You Speak, You Become

We've already covered the idea that each food holds its own vibrational frequency, and when a food is consumed, it becomes a part of the being who is consuming it. Well, thoughts and words are no different. Every thought you think and every word you speak also holds its own vibration. The vibration of each thought and word, just like the vibration of food, is what makes up the vibration of an individual on both the physical and spiritual levels of being. For this reason, what you think and what you speak, you become. The following is a short excerpt from a chapter in my book entitled *The Language of Energy*, in which I include an in-depth explanation regarding the power of one's speech:

> *"The words that come out of one's mouth have immense power. Each word has its own energetic blueprint that resonates with a specific reality. One should never speak a word that they don't want to manifest into their life, not even as a joke. It may sound funny, but this is very important. Once again, every word has an energetic blueprint, and by speaking a word, one inherits its energetic blueprint. Just like one wouldn't consume poison because it will physically harm them, why would one inherit a poison that will energetically harm them?"*

Ultimately, the words one speaks are reflective of the thoughts they think. With this idea in mind, we understand that both thought and speech are very powerful tools that can be used in a beneficial way to help lift one's vibration. However, these tools can also be used in a detrimental way to lower one's vibration and, therefore, block the divine light and spiritual abundance from coming down into the dimensions of the body, mind, spirit, and soul.

"The Evil Tongue"

Speech can be used as a medium to express low, and in some cases even dangerous, vibrations. In Hebrew, there is a type of derogatory speech known as *lashon hara*. *Lashon hara*, otherwise known as "evil tongue," is a term for derogatory speech about a person, which damages or lowers that person in the view of others. *Lashon hara* is a dangerous and detrimental way to use one's speech since it doesn't affect only the individual who is expressing the low-vibrational speech, but also the individual toward whom these words are being expressed.

As a matter of fact, using speech to express low-vibrational energy such as *lashon hara* can actually make the speaker physically sick, with the sickness being expressed through skin issues. The following is a lengthy excerpt from *Rays of Light*, which documents a dialogue between Rabbi AA and Ray where Rabbi AA is teaching Ray about the dangers of *lashon hara*. The rabbi uses Ray as a firsthand example of what the consequences of using speech in a derogatory way can be. Please note that when Rabbi AA refers to "leprosy," he is not only referring to the individual skin disease, but to all types of skin diseases:

> ***Rabbi AA:*** *Out of my love to you, I will just warn you in regards to the subject of lashon hara. If you were to sit and learn, you would understand that leprosy came into this*

world through lashon hara. You know and understand that everything works and moves by means of different energies within our universe. God is energy. We are all energy. There are different energies, however, we are all one. One energy. You must understand and embrace that lashon hara is a type of negative energy that blocks the divine light (God) from reaching us. The word tzaraat in Hebrew (leprosy, in English) *is a general word for different skin diseases. Rest assured that each person who suffers from specific skin issues is contaminated with lashon hara. More lashon hara equates to more skin problems and illness. And when does a person speak lashon hara? Only when he falls into the ego net and puts himself in the center. The mouth was intended for praising and exalting the Creator and his creations and to please mankind. We are forbidden to speak through pride, rather only from love.*

Ray: *I don't think there exists a person who hasn't occupied themselves with lashon hara before.*

Rabbi AA: *Maybe you're right, but the difference is in the level of lashon hara and its purpose. There is a difference between people who realize their mistakes and immediately correct themselves to people who are not even willing to admit/acknowledge the injustice that they are causing to themselves and others through their words. Look around you at your friends and family who suffer from skin conditions. Examine their actions and their ways and you will understand that I am right. Lashon hara is an energy that influences the giver and the receiver as well. Look into your soul and your body. You yourself have had skin issues on your face for almost one year now. Ask yourself, when did it begin? And why? Ask yourself why you aren't able to solve* *the problem when it apparently seems to be very simple. You've asked me, many different doctors, and tried different medicines but nothing seems to work. Maybe you should begin asking yourself questions? May you should be more aware of your filthy mouth? Maybe you should speak less and think more? Maybe you should find a way to correct the lashon hara that you have planted throughout the years? I hope you are not thinking of denying the lashon hara that comes out of your mouth?*

Ray: *No, I am not denying it. When I see something wrong and not fair or just, I simply want to bring the truth to light.*

Rabbi AA: *There is no problem to bring the truth to light and speak truth. There is a problem that through your words and expressions, you turn light into darkness.*

Ray: All right. I understand. Let me think about it.

This excerpt is a direct and firsthand example of how speech, a tool that has the power to spiritually lift us up, can be used in a way that lowers our individual vibration of being and damages the physical body. On the other hand, using the mouth and one's speech to express vibrations of gratitude and love will not only positively impact us on all levels of being, but will also create more energetic alignment and flow within us, thus providing a more compatible instrument for the divine light to flow through on all levels of being (body, mind, spirit, and soul). Scientific studies have been conducted to show the true power and impact that both positive and negative thoughts, words, and intentions have not only on us, but on everything around us as well.

Masaru Emoto was a Japanese businessman, author, and scientist who claimed that our thoughts, words, and intentions impact the physical realm. His studies were focused on the evidence of how the molecular structure of water transforms when it is exposed to specific words, thoughts, sounds, and intentions. Based on his research, he found that when water was exposed to loving and compassionate intentions and words, the molecular formation of the water when observed under a microscope became symmetrical and aesthetically pleasing. On the other hand, when the water was exposed to low-vibrational thoughts, words, and intentions in alignment with fear, discord, division, and disharmony, the molecular formation of the water when observed under a microscope was disconnected, disfigured, and distorted. The following pictures are directly from his studies. The intention, thoughts, and/or words that were used on the water in each experiment are directly under each picture:

Love and Gratitude

You Disgust Me

Evil

Thank You

Eternal

Peace

It is important to remember that the human body
is comprised of 70 percent water. We have already
established that the body is the root that influences

the layers that are above it (mind, spirit, and soul). We've also learned that when the body is ready and pure, it will elevate. But if the body is faulty and corrupt, the receiving of spiritual abundance will be sealed, blocked, hidden, and buried.

It is evident, from Masaru Emoto and his studies with water, that thoughts, words, and intentions impact the structure of the water that makes up the majority of our bodies, which therefore affects both the physical and spiritual health of the body. This means that thoughts, words, and intentions have the ability to keep the body in a pure state while also being able to bring illness and disease upon the body. Ultimately, depending upon the way we use these tools and instruments, we can either purify and elevate the body to a higher level of awareness in order to receive spiritual abundance, or we can corrupt the body and therefore lower our vibration of being, thus blocking our ability to receive spiritual abundance.

The Power of Faith

Faith is defined as the complete trust or confidence in someone or something. Ultimately, it is the undoubted belief in the divine light (God) based on spiritual apprehension rather than proof. The following excerpt is from *Rays of Light*. In this excerpt, Rabbi AA speaks about the importance of faith, how disease is an expression of a foundational lack of faith, and how faith can be regained:

> ***Rabbi AA:*** *The essence of our diseases is rooted in a flaw within the essence of our faith. This means that our medicine and healing consist of regaining our faith. Matzah is the bread of faith, which is the first most medicinal bread. It used to be customary in the Holy Temple of the Jewish people to sacrifice the manna and the matzah together along with all of the first fruits of Shavuot* (a Jewish holiday) *for the remembrance of*

the power of faith and the power of prayer as well as the heavenly power of godliness that resides within us. By sacrifice, I mean that the high priests would simply eat the manna and the matzah. The matzah is the food of faith, which empowers the soul with the light of faith. Prior to everything, one needs faith. Faith is the root of everything. Without faith there is nothing.

Ray: *Just for the record, I don't agree with you regarding faith.*

Rabbi AA: *I really appreciate what's in your heart. Let us continue. The matzah symbolizes faith, freedom, and happiness. Pay attention, you personally don't like to eat matzah, and you barely touch matzah on Passover.*

Ray: *So, what? It's just fattening and causes constipation.*

Rabbi AA: You have no faith, including the fact that you have no faith in yourself. You complain that you are handcuffed and that your freedom was taken away from you by your children, your family, your business, etc., and due to your lack of freedom you feel frustrated and sad. You're looking for excuses and reasons to explain your dissipated happiness. You insist on meeting with God and all to improve your situation, your joy and your happiness.

Ray: So, what you're trying to tell me is that I need to eat more matzah and not try to meet with God?

Rabbi AA: Maybe you will suddenly realize that your children are freedom and happiness and not a burden or a task. He who gets it will understand, and he who doesn't is a fool.

Ray: I don't remember you eating matzah.

Rabbi AA: Always, providing that the matzah is kosher, clean, pure, and unblemished.

Ray: All right, can we move on? I promise to eat a lot of matzah next Passover.

Rabbi AA: Strengthen your faith.

Ray: Okay, I'll work on it.

My intention in bringing forth this excerpt from *Rays of Light* is to show how the lack of faith can negatively impact the body, as well as what tools can be used in order to reverse this lack of faith and renew the health of the body. As we can understand from the excerpt above, Ray's lack of faith has ultimately led him to a place where he holds low-vibrational thoughts. These thoughts have led to his body housing distorted and unstructured water, which has affected the physical health of his body, thus blocking his ability to attain a higher level of awareness and to receive spiritual abundance. Ultimately, the lack of faith creates an unhealthy body, and thus blocks one's ability to receive the divine light and spiritual abundance.

As we've already established, the reality we experience is a reflection of the vibrations we are in resonance with. Although the current collective level of awareness is quite low, we have endless tools and resources at our disposal to make a positive shift on the collective level. These tools include the knowledge behind the power of food, the knowledge behind the power of thought and speech, and the knowledge behind the power of faith. However, the foundation of using these tools lies in the understanding that they all help purify the body because the body is the base that must be pure in order to elevate and reach higher levels of awareness on all levels of being (body, mind, spirit, and soul).

After all, in order to attain a high level of awareness and receive spiritual abundance, one must be spiritually healthy—and in order to be spiritually healthy, one must be physically healthy.

FIFTH-DIMENSIONAL AWARENESS

We are multi-dimensional beings. Although we currently experience life on the collective level through third-dimensional awareness, we are not limited to third-dimensional awareness. In third-dimensional awareness, we do not hold a true awareness of the interconnectivity between all things and all beings in the universe. We hold illusory beliefs that keep us in a lower-vibrational matrix. In other words, staying in third-dimensional awareness and consciousness handicaps our energetic and spiritual abilities. Illusions such as time, separation, and death, among many others, must first be understood as illusions and not fundamental realities in order to begin the ascension process to higher levels of awareness.

Once we succeed in dissolving these illusions, we become liberated from the enslavement to lower levels of awareness, therefore allowing us to reach the higher dimensions. First and foremost, we must understand the different dimensions that exists and how they work. Once we understand this concept, progressing to higher dimensions will become easier.

10 Dimensions

The universe and everything it is made up of—both tangible and intangible, including us—is comprised of ten different dimensions (not including "Dimension X" where shapeshifters operate). I have only been given the names of the first five: beta, alpha, theta, delta, and gamma. Modern science has identified these dimensions as brain wave frequencies on the physical level of understanding. It is important to understand that modern science can study only what it can measure through its physical instruments. If it lacks tools and instruments to measure something, it cannot understand it or verify it. This is why science calls anything having to do with spirituality a "pseudoscience," because spiritual phenomena surpass the limitations of what our current scientific system has the ability to understand.

Modern science does not understand the true significance and meaning of what these dimensions, which scientists call brain wave frequencies, truly are because they are limited to the study of physical phenomena, whereas the true power to understand these dimensions lies within spiritual phenomena. However, these are not simple brain wave patterns, rather they are different dimensions, which translate to different levels of awareness.

Each dimension is broken up into 10 different portions, for example, beta-1, beta-2, beta-3, all the way to beta-10. Another example would be gamma-4, gamma-5, Gamma-6, and so on. Each dimension has its own traits, characteristics, beliefs, and abilities associated with it. The lower dimensions, such as beta, are more in resonance with the physical and material world, whereas the higher dimensions, such as gamma, are more in resonance with the spiritual and energetic world. Actions such as levitation, flight with the body, and telepathic communication are very natural in higher states of dimensional awareness such as the upper levels of gamma.

However, these same actions are considered impossible at lower states of dimensional awareness such as beta—and rightfully so, because in order to have accessibility to such abilities, one must be in resonance with a high state of dimensional awareness, such as the upper levels of gamma. As a matter of fact, the reason why Rabbi AA, and many others, have access to such incredible abilities that humanity (on the collective level) would consider supernatural is because he possessed a very high-dimensional awareness that was in alignment with the upper levels of gamma.

Measuring Dimensional Awareness

Everyone is born with a specific state of dimensional awareness. Some are born on the upper levels of delta, or even gamma, while others are born on lower levels of alpha, or even beta. Most of humanity is currently in the lower dimensions of awareness, which mainly corresponds to the vibrational range of lower levels of beta through alpha. In "The Pyramid Code," it states the following:

> *"We, humans, are the lowest level of conscious-ness before plants. Even animals have sur-passed us. Humans today are at an extremely low level, far from the fifth dimension."*

There are different techniques that can be used to measure one's level of dimensional awareness, and I have been privileged to experience one of them myself firsthand with Ray. This occurred about a year ago, when Ray was teaching me about the different dimensions, how they work, and what they mean. I understood that Rabbi AA taught him how to measure one's state of dimensional awareness, so I asked him if he could measure mine, and so he did.

The name of the technique Ray used on me is called the "fetal position technique." This technique allows the reader to read the state of dimensional awareness that one was born with, along with one's current state of dimensional awareness. It was quite an interesting experience that lasted roughly 10 minutes or so. I was lying down on my left side in a fetal position, and Ray was lying behind me with his stomach on my back as his body molded around my body (he was in a fetal position as well).

Every so often, Ray would press against my forehead with both the index and middle finger of his right hand (right around the area of the third eye). Throughout the process, he would tense up and even pull his hand away, since he felt strong currents of electricity coming out of my forehead and the back of my neck. According to Ray, I was born with a state of dimensional awareness that corresponds to the upper levels of delta (delta-8). However, I was at a state of dimensional awareness that corresponds to the upper levels of alpha when Ray read me through the fetal position technique. Depending upon how one lives their life, which includes the food they eat, the words they speak, the amount of stress they hold, and so on, one can either increase or decrease their state of dimensional awareness relative to the state of dimensional awareness that they were born with.

Over the past couple of years, I have been working on purifying my body in order to heal the damage that I have done thus far, with the intention of bringing myself back to the state of dimensional awareness I was born with, the upper levels of delta, at a minimum. I am currently being guided in order to reach this new level of personal awareness. Some of my instructions include staying away from the inhalation of any kind of smoke, steering clear of the consumption of alcohol, and keeping a clean vegan diet in order to reclaim the power I was born with.

Just as Ray wrote in *The Pyramid Code*, "So long as we live in a limited and impure body, with a limited mind and a closed heart, we will not be able to reach the level of consciousness I am writing about (the fifth dimension or higher)."

Understanding Fifth-Dimensional Awareness

So, what is fifth-dimensional awareness, and why is it so necessary for us to reach it? First, fifth-dimensional awareness is the awareness that we must reach on a collective level through the universe in order to enter the Age of Love. Ultimately, possessing fifth-dimensional awareness is no different than being in resonance with the gamma dimension. This is because the gamma dimension *is* the fifth dimension. Fifth-dimensional awareness allows us to truly understand, not just conceptually, but also through application and experience, that life is consciousness and consciousness is life, therefore dissolving the illusion of "death."

It allows us to truly understand that the divine light (God) is not the creator, but the very source of creation itself. It allows us to truly understand that the divine light is not some separate, superior, and condemning entity that most religious institutions claim it to be. It allows us to understand that by believing that the divine light is something external from ourselves, we separate ourselves from the source and immediately become limited beings.

In fifth-dimensional awareness, we completely understand and know that there is *one* unified field of consciousness that connects all beings and all things in the universe, therefore dissolving the illusion of "separation." It allows us to truly understand and know through firsthand experience that the divine light (God), which is the source of all creation in the universe, exists within everything and every being. Once we reach fifth-dimensional awareness on a collective level, realities such as evil, corruption, division, greed, and war will no longer exist.

The attainment of fifth-dimensional awareness will dissolve any limiting and false beliefs we currently possess, further unifying humanity and the universe as a whole. In other words, when we reach fifth-dimensional awareness, all our physical and spiritual limitations will be stripped away, and we will be granted spiritual freedom, just like the advanced extraterrestrial beings who are among us today. After all, fifth-dimensional awareness is the reason why extraterrestrials had, and still have, access to such high and "supernatural" abilities.

The following excerpt is from "The Pyramid Code," and shows the true power of fifth-dimensional awareness. Please note that Fatasol is the pharaonic name of the extraterrestrial race that settled in ancient Egypt in the year 2750 BC, according to the document:

> "Although Fatasol were housed in a physical body, they were granted perfect spiritual freedom, which completely liberated them from time and space. Because of this divine consciousness, they could move freely, between stars and galaxies, without the influence of time or space. In other words, they were able to experience the past, present, and future simultaneously. This means that if we are released from the limitations of time and space by true and pure spiritual consciousness, we can lead ourselves through our consciousness as our soul desires (whether it is to a physical or a spiritual place). This is done through the purification of the body, the mind, the spirit, and the soul. In such a state of consciousness,

within the fifth dimension (in a state of gamma or higher), we can reach even higher levels of being just like the original Fatasol of the original divine race and pure offspring used to do. Their capabilities had no physical or spiritual limitations. For them, there is no such thing as "here" or "there" or "we" or "they." They were able to differentiate between different perspectives of the one and only reality, which is the beingness that everything is eternal, everything is now, everything is here, everything is one, and we are all one. This is the divine consciousness of the fifth dimension or higher. This consciousness even today will bring us to the highest places."

This excerpt shows us not only the power we can access once we reach fifth-dimensional awareness, but it also gives us insights into some of what must be done in order to reach this level of awareness. First of all, it teaches us that these high-vibrational beings were *"granted perfect spiritual freedom which completely liberated them from time and space."* The reason why they were able to *"move freely between stars and galaxies without the influence of time or space"* is because they didn't have limiting belief systems, as we do. Our current collective belief system, which is in alignment with the awareness of the beta dimension, limits us.

Because we are so preoccupied with the physical and material world, we believe that time and space actually exist as we perceive them. However, if we were able to transcend our collective low level of awareness to dimensions above that of beta awareness, we would begin to become more preoccupied with the spiritual instead of the material, and therefore we would begin to think in terms of energy, frequency, and vibration. In doing so, we would clearly understand that time is not a fundamental reality, but a relative reality.

There is no other moment than the present moment. In order to travel distances in "no-time," it is not enough to just conceptually understand that time does not exist in the way that we perceive it. We must transcend to higher states of dimensional awareness, such as gamma (the fifth dimension), in order to be able to truly experience our current conceptual knowingness of no-time, therefore dissolving the illusion of time. Additionally, this excerpt also reiterates that the body must be pure in order to elevate spiritually when it says, *"this is done through the purification of the body, the mind, the spirit, and the soul."*

Seeing is Believing

With such grand claims regarding "supernatural" abilities, unrivaled technology, extraterrestrial life, and the like, many people want to "see the proof." As a matter of fact, one of the big reasons why Ray was, and is still, not willing to step up and reveal himself along with the information that he holds is because TLS has not allowed him to reveal the codes to unlock the information, which is where all the proof resides. The more I think about why TLS would do such a thing, the more I understand, and even agree, with their decision. The answers exist within the information and the excerpts brought forth into this book from "The Pyramid Code" and *Rays of Light*.

The first question that must be asked is: What is proof? Proof is defined as the evidence that establishes or helps one to establish a fact or the truth of a statement. However, is there truly such a thing as definite proof? If Ray or Rabbi AA were to levitate in front of your eyes, would you believe it then? What if the head of the New York chapter of TLS were to shapeshift into a dog in front of your eyes, would you believe it then? Well, we know that illusionists such as David Copperfield have "levitated" in front of thousands of people. He even made the Statue of Liberty "disappear" in front of millions of people. However, we know his alleged abilities are simply illusions to the eye.

So, I will ask you again—is there truly such thing as definite proof? Is there any sort of proof that could be brought forth that nobody would be able to refute without any sort of potential explanation or excuse as to why the proof is not sufficient? If Ray or Rabbi AA levitated before your eyes, who is to say they are not illusionists as well? Even if the head of the New York chapter of TLS were to shapeshift before your eyes, who is to say that you were not drugged and simply experienced a hallucination? Ultimately, there is no such thing as definite proof. For some people, trusted individuals conveying their personal experiences are sufficient proof. For others, pictures and videos are sufficient proof. There are those who require physical experiences for sufficient proof.

And believe it or not, there are those who experience all of the above and still do not believe what they are seeing. So, although many people think seeing is believing, is it? The burden of proof is not contingent on the evidence that one can see, but rather on one's willingness to believe, coupled with the extent to which one is willing to let go of their current beliefs and adopt new ones based on their knowledge and experience.

The significance of fifth-dimensional awareness when it comes to the idea of proof is that, in such a high level of awareness, we gain the ability to perceive certain things that we are not able to see in our current collective level of awareness. In order to understand why this is so, we must first understand what perception is.

Our range of perception is dictated by our level of awareness. The higher our state of dimensional awareness, the more we are able to perceive.

Ultimately, our collective range of perception is infinitesimally small compared to the infinite range of frequencies that make up the universe. If something exists outside our range of perception/ awareness, it can be right in front of our eyes and we will not be able to see it. In other words, if one's state of dimensional awareness is in beta, they will not be able to perceive anything that exists in the dimension of gamma because it is not within their range of perception (awareness).

This means that just because you don't see something with your eyes does not mean it doesn't exist. For example, we know that there are microwaves traveling around us all the time. Although we can't see them, we know they exist because we have certain tools that allow us to perceive their existence and therefore measure them. The reason we can't see these microwaves, although they exist, is because they exist outside our range of perception (awareness). The following excerpt from "The Pyramid Code" is a direct and present-day example of how something can be right in front of our eyes, yet our level of awareness (perception) hinders us from seeing it:

> "The Zodiac constantly emits 12 different energies from its 12 different, fixed constellations in the direction of Earth. Within the confines of each of the 12 constellations of the Zodiac exist 12 stars that are not visible to those who are not currently at the awareness of the upper levels of the fifth dimension (gamma) or higher. Each of the 12 stars within the confines of each constellation spins on its own axis. Additionally, the 12 stars within the confines of each constellation all revolve around the center of each constellation as a unit. This means that there are 144 stars within the confines of the constellations in the Zodiac that are not visible to the eye. These stars will only become visible to us when we reach the upper limits of the fifth dimension (gamma) or higher."

The reason why we will be able to see these stars only when we reach fifth-dimensional awareness (gamma or higher) is because these stars exist in the fifth dimension, and in order to be aware of them, we must be in resonance with the fifth dimension. This is a prime example of something that is right in front of our eyes that we are not able to see— not because it doesn't exist, but because our current collective range of perception, and therefore our level of awareness—is limited to dimensions that are below the dimensions that those stars exist on.

Where is the Proof?

Proof already exists. The question is, why can't we see it? As Rabbi AA stated in *Rays of Light*, *"The divine light (God) is not revealed without the proper tools and instruments to receive it."* The receiving of proof is very much like the receiving of the divine light. We know that the body must be prepared in order to receive spiritual abundance. It works the same way when it comes to proof. We must prepare ourselves in order to be "ready" for the receiving of proof. And the preparation consists of the purification of the body, mind, spirit, and soul. What "ready" means in this context is simply coming into resonance with the proof in order to attain the ability to see it.

In other words, proof will not be revealed without the proper awareness to receive it. In this case, the word "revealed" does not imply that proof is being withheld from us from an external source, but rather that we are withholding the revelation of proof from ourselves, simply by not being in resonance with it. Ultimately, we will not be able to see the proof as proof in the first place until we are in resonance with it. For this reason, awareness is the key to unlocking the limitless potential and power and receiving the spiritual abundance and the divine light (God) that resides within each and every one of us.

I believe that as we climb the dimensional ladder of awareness, we will come to realize that the proof was in front of us the whole time, and the only reason we couldn't see it is because we were not in resonance with it and therefore, we were not ready to receive it. The beautiful thing about this revelation is that it allows us to understand that preparing ourselves to be ready for the receiving of spiritual abundance and the divine light (God) is completely our responsibility. TLS is simply helping to guide and prepare us to receive what has been around us and within us all along!

A Future of Knowledge and Awareness

At this point, the true significance of knowledge, and therefore awareness, should be more apparent. We have learned that knowledge and awareness are the keys to reaching higher levels of consciousness on the collective level, and therefore creating a positive shift in the reality we experience. Ultimately, knowledge and awareness are the keys that grant us access to making our world a better place, simply because the reality we experience is a direct reflection of the level of dimensional awareness we possess on the collective level.

I have done my best to shed light on the sacred knowledge and mysticism that have been hidden from us for millennia by bringing forth insights from "The Pyramid Code," excerpts from *Rays of Light*, information I have received from Ray and TLS, and personal experiences I have had the honor of receiving over the past few years.

I look forward to reading and digesting the new information from *Rays of Light* that I was given to read on October 10, 2020 (10/10/2020). From the day I received the papers to read, Ray said over and over again, "You can read it whenever you'd like, but I suggest you wait." Although I went through phases of frustration, I ultimately listened to his guidance and held off.

Today, I feel a lot more prepared to read the papers. I feel that through the writing of this book, I reached a new level of awareness that will help me understand the new information I am about to read with much more clarity and transparency. My hope is that after I read and fully digest the information, I will be able to write a second part to this book with even more insights and knowledge, with the intention of helping guide us all in reaching a higher level of awareness and consciousness, and ultimately bringing us closer to the Age of Love.

I would like to express my utmost gratitude to Ray, TLS, and the universe as a whole for granting me access to such incredible knowledge and mysticism. Moreover, I would like to thank the divine light for guiding me through this process of disclosure.

Although it may feel lonely and overwhelming at times, I know that I am never alone.

We are all on our own individual paths of revealing and realizing the fullest potential of limitless and eternal divine power that resides within each and every one of us. We are *one*, and the day is coming where we will truly experience this concept on a collective level. May we come together, may we unite, and may we reach new levels of awareness and consciousness with the intention to create the positive shift that humanity, and all life in the universe, deserves!

I wish you all a beautiful journey of self-discovery and personal awareness filled with light, peace, and love.

Printed in Great Britain
by Amazon

16431862R00149